THE
MADNESS OF KING GEORGE

THE INGENIOUS INSANTIY OF OUR MOST "MISUNDERESTIMATED" PRESIDENT

MICHAEL K. SMITH & MATT WUERKER

Common Courage Press   Monroe, Maine

ISBN 1-56751-248-8 paper
ISBN 1-56751-249-6 cloth

Library of Congress Cataloguing in Publication.
Data is available from the publisher.

Common Courage Press
121 Red Barn Road
Monroe, ME 04951
(800) 497-3207
commoncouragepress.com

Printed in Canada, First printing

madness, n. 1. Insanity. 2. Great folly: *"O madness, to think use of strongest wines / And strongest drinks our chief support of health."* (Milton). 3. Fury, rage: *"But the hunger madness made them terrifying, irresistible."* (Jack London). 4. Enthusiasm: excitement.— See Synonyms at **insanity**.

—The American Heritage Dictionary
of the English Language

TABLE OF CONTENTS

FOREWORD

I'M LOSING MY PATIENCE WITH MY NEIGHBORS, MR. BUSH

I'm really excited by George Bush's latest reason for bombing Iraq: he's running out of patience. And so am I!

For some time now I've been really pissed off with Mr. Johnson, who lives a couple of doors down the street. Well, him and Mr. Patel, who runs the health food shop. They both give me queer looks, and I'm sure Mr. Johnson is planning something nasty for me, but so far I haven't been able to discover what. I've been round to his place a few times to see what he's up to, but he's got everything well hidden. That's how devious he is.

As for Mr. Patel, don't ask me how I know, I just know - from very good sources - that he is, in reality, a Mass Murderer. I have leafleted the street telling them that if we don't act first, he'll pick us off one by one.

Some of my neighbours say, if I've got proof, why don't I go to the police? But that's simply ridiculous. The police will say that they need evidence of a crime with which to charge my neighbors.

They'll come up with endless red tape and quibbling about the rights and wrongs of a pre-emptive strike and all the while Mr. Johnson will be finalising his plans to do terrible things to me, while Mr. Patel will be secretly murdering people. Since I'm the only one in the street with a decent range of automatic firearms, I reckon it's up to me to keep the peace. But until recently that's been a little difficult. Now, however, George W. Bush has made it clear that all I need to do is run out of patience, and then I can wade in and do whatever I want!

And let's face it, Mr. Bush's carefully thought-out policy towards Iraq is the only way to bring about international peace and security. The one certain way to stop Muslim fundamentalist suicide bombers targeting the US or the UK is to bomb a few Muslim countries that have never threatened us.

That's why I want to blow up Mr. Johnson's garage and kill his wife and children. Strike first! That'll teach him a lesson. Then he'll leave us in peace and stop peering at me in that totally unacceptable way.

Mr. Bush makes it clear that all he needs to know before bombing Iraq is that Saddam is a really nasty man and that he has weapons of mass destruction even if no one can find them. I'm certain I've just as much justification for killing Mr. Johnson's wife and children as Mr. Bush has for bombing Iraq. Mr. Bush's long-term aim is to make the world a safer place by eliminating 'rogue states' and 'terrorism.' It's such a clever long-term aim because how can you ever know when you've achieved it? How will Mr. Bush know when he's wiped out all terrorists? When every single terrorist is dead? But then a terrorist is only a terrorist once he's committed an act of terror. What about would-be terrorists? These are the ones you really want to eliminate, since most of the known terrorists, being suicide bombers, have already eliminated themselves.

Perhaps Mr. Bush needs to wipe out everyone who could possibly be a future terrorist? Maybe he can't be sure he's achieved his objective until every Muslim fundamentalist is dead? But then some moderate Muslims might convert to fundamentalism. Maybe the only really safe thing to do would be for Mr. Bush to eliminate all Muslims?

It's the same in my street. Mr. Johnson and Mr. Patel are just the tip of the iceberg. There are dozens of other people in the street who I don't like and who - quite frankly - look at me in odd ways. No one will be really safe until I've wiped them all out.

My wife says I might be going too far but I tell her I'm simply using the same logic as the President of the United States. That shuts her up.

Like Mr. Bush, I've run out of patience, and if that's a good enough reason for the President, it's good enough for me. I'm going to give the whole street two weeks - no, 10 days - to come out in the open and hand over all aliens and interplanetary hijackers, galactic outlaws and interstellar terrorist masterminds, and if they don't hand them over nicely and say 'Thank you,' I'm going to bomb the entire street to kingdom come.

It's just as sane as what George W. Bush is proposing - and, in contrast to what he's intending, my policy will destroy only one street.

Terry Jones
The Guardian
Sunday January 26, 2003

INTRODUCTION

Bush, like Moses, is a leadership genius.

—Carolyn B. Thompson and James B. Ware,
The Leadership Genius of George W. Bush

No other president can match his record of effortless achievement, which extends back farther than most people realize.

It began with selecting the right parents, insuring he would be born rich. With steely discipline he then trained himself to advance along the path of no resistance, receiving the imprimatur of Ivy League schools, avoiding service in Vietnam, getting bailed out of failed West Texas oil companies, profiting off a Harken Energy insider-trading deal, receiving the Texas Rangers for being the President's son, acquiring the land to build the team a new stadium by improper use of eminent domain, winning the Texas governorship trading on the family name, amassing a record financial war-chest exploiting Dad's GOP connections, gaining the White House through a Florida vote rigged by his brother, and inheriting limitless political capital from the most devastating terrorist attack in American history. Few can doubt this record places him in very select company indeed.

Which is not to say that outstanding public servants haven't graced the Oval Office in the past, and rather frequently at that. As the eminent presidential historian George Carlin has pointed out, the last eight presidents of the 20th century were of uniformly excellent character: "A hillbilly with a permanent hard-on; an upper-class bureaucrat-twit, an actor-imbecile, a born-again Christian peanut farmer, an unelected college football lineman, a paranoid moral dwarf, a vulgar cowboy criminal, and a mediocre playboy sex fiend."

But George W. Bush has distinguished himself even in this exclusive company, quickly surpassing the achievements of all of his august predecessors. Who among them, for example, ever thought of forcing a nation to disarm and then attacking it? I dare say such a brilliant strategy would not have occurred to any ordinary mind, which just goes to show you what a war-mongering deserter-drunk can do once determined to rid the world of evil.

In the exciting pages ahead you will read of this living legend's meteoric rise from Trust Fund baby to King of the Planet, of elections bought and stolen; of an All-Star Cabinet making the world safe for global oil barons; of our defective Constitution and why we no longer need it; of the call for secret tribunals and clandestine executions and why we do need them; of tax cuts for needy billionaires and tough love for the greedy poor; of eternal war and its blissful consequences; of astronomical budget deficits breeding prosperity for all; of looted surpluses, gutted benefits, and plundered stocks paving the way for a better America; of mini-nukes and maxi-carnage; of American presidents using WMD for noble purposes and of gutsy advice on surviving WMD attacks launched by former clients; of the seven habits of highly effective Empires; of parents selling blood plasma to fund their children's education; of corporate swindling for fun and profit; and most importantly, of the deep humanism animating Bushevik ideology and practice. In short, you will bear witness to our onward march to utopia behind the most inspired leadership in US history.

As we approach the earthly paradise let us express our profound gratitude that Bush delivered on his promise to restore integrity to the White House, making us proud and respected again. Be forewarned that when familiarizing yourself with the awesome accomplishments that flowed from this singular transformation, you probably won't be able to resist the temptation to send him your life savings. This is only to be expected. For when a man takes it upon himself to bless the world with compassionate conservatism, it is only natural that we feel moved to do everything we can to help out.

As the president constantly reminds us, only evildoers can possibly think otherwise.

CHAPTER ONE

SILVER SPOONS AND GOLDEN HANDSHAKES

GREASED SKIDS TO GREATNESS

You Might Ask Yourself…

You might ask yourself, Why George W. Bush? Why this man… at this time? How were we this lucky? It's a big question.

As the new millennium dawned the United States found itself teetering, in more ways than anyone ever imagined, on the edge of a brand new era. In the election of 2000 the American people were not to be distracted by a booming economy, the first federal budget surplus in decades, and silly talk about a peace dividend. The great American public, whipped into a lather by a scandal-wracked media was hell-bent on doing something about returning integrity, honesty, and dignity to the White House.

When it came to the first presidential election of the new century, with the nation clamoring for change, at this auspicious juncture—in rides a humble cowboy from Midland Texas. As in other pivotal moments in the upward march of civilization history works in mysterious ways. And as fate would have it, destiny intervenes (as well as the Supreme Court) and provides a man for the moment. A man whose grasp of history, world affairs, not to mention the english language has been greatly misunderestimated.

Was it just dumb luck for us and the world? This natural born leader on a white horse, the one branded with a crooked "E", arriving at this seminal moment in history will surely shape the future in ways none of us can imagine.

They say people get the leaders they deserve. Then the question arises, "At a moment like this, what did we do to deserve a leader like this?"

The Boot-Strapping Story of an Average Guy from Midland Texas

1946 — Before being transplanted to his hard scrabble beginnings in Midland Texas, GW Bush is actually sprouted on July 6 just off campus from Yale University in New Haven Connecticut. Born under a lucky star that cynics dismiss as one of privilege, family and his family's values will always be important to GW.

The rugged "pull yourself up by your own boot straps" individualism of the great American meritocracy into which he was so fortunately born is instilled at an early age in young GW.

Grandpa Prescott Bush and maternal grandfather George Herbert Walker were the forces behind the Brown Brothers Harriman, the largest private banking house of its time on Wall Street, which specialized in US-German trade before and during the boom years of the Third Reich. His will becomes a powerful US Senator.

Yale is more than a birthplace for GW. It's the alma mater of both his father and his grandfather. The Bush legacy also extends to Yale's secretive and exclusive Skull and Bones Society into which many of the Bush men of several generations will be inducted.

1958 — Like so many brave pioneers before them, GHW Bush and Barbara pack up their family and head west to pursue work as oil executives. With the combination of determination and good luck that will become a hallmark of the Bush family's secret to success, GW's Dad rises quickly. Through hard work and perseverance GHW Bush manages to kick and scrape his way up the ladder of an oil equipment company in Midland, Texas whose parent company is Dresser Industries, a conglomerate that just happens to also have his Dad on it's board of directors.

> *"Midland was Yuppieland west."*
> —George HW Bush

1959 — GW's common roots and humble upbringing lasts through the eighth grade in Midland's public schools. GW then leaves Midland for the fancy Kinkaid School in Houston. Early in his stint at Kinkaid it's clear that he is a natural leader of men as he demonstrates a prowess at sports and wins his first election as a class officer.

1961 — GW's packed off to Phillips Academy in Andover; despite quickly finding himself at the bottom of his class academically GW finds his niche. He becomes a cheerleader.

1962 — Showing his typical moxie, he rises quickly through the ranks and becomes Andover's head cheerleader. Assuming these heavy responsibilities his interest in the exercise of political power begins to stir. He demands 100% senior attendance at Andover-Exeter games. One season those who don't show up are hissed at by the entire class and pelted with milk cartons in the food line. Even the acne-faced "losers" join in. GW's leadership abilities becoming evident.

1964 — GW enrolls at Yale. Rejecting the morally corrupt counter culture and the degenerate anti-war movement, he prefers mixing screwdrivers in a garbage can before football games—just another one of his character building responsibilities as president of Delta Kappa Epsilon fraternity.

Showing a knack for keeping priorities straight GW will later reflect, "I don't remember any kind of heaviness ruining my time at Yale." Meanwhile, Yale student leaders get sidetracked by political correctness, signing an Ivy League manifesto saying they are "seriously considering or have already decided to leave the country or go to jail rather than serve in Vietnam."

1966 — Foreshadowing his future strong Christian beliefs, GW's busted for stealing a wreath during Holiday season. Charges dropped.

With the draft looming, GW calls classmate Robert Birge a "chickenshit" for not signing up for Vietnam.

1967 — GW's plans to marry Cathryn Lee Wolfman announced in *Houston Chronicle* society column. Wedding called off, say friends, due to "nasty, snobbish whispers" about the young woman's "merchant" family.

GW enmeshed in fraternity scandal over initiating new members with "branding." *Yale Daily News* editorializes: "Initiations, formal or informal, which are brutal or degrading in any way have no place in a recognized undergraduate activity." GW standing on tradition, tells *NY Times* that the practice involves "only a cigarette burn."

1968—The war against the Vietnamese rages on. Having nothing whatsoever to do with it being a sure-fire way to avoid fighting in Vietnam, and no doubt having more to do with love of country, there is a waiting list of 100,000 Texans hoping to get into the Texas National Guard.

Filled with patriotic zeal (and with just days remaining on his student deferment) GW manages to enlist in the Texas Air National Guard. Emblematic of "the luck of the Bushes" and despite a score of 25% on a pilot aptitude test (the absolute numerical minimum) GW miraculously vaults over 500 other applicants to get one of a handful of pilot slots. Daddy, who happens to be a Congress member from Texas, hurries to have his picture taken with his patriotic son in a military uniform.

" I have no idea and don't believe so"

—George W. Bush, when asked if strings were pulled to get him into the Texas National Guard— thus avoiding the draft

GW attends flight training school in Valdosta, Georgia. Overflowing with gratitude to at last be fighting to defend the frontiers of the free world, he spends Friday nights partying hard at the Officers Club, more than once stripping off his uniform and dancing nude atop the bar while lip-synching to jukebox tunes.

1970 — GW finishes pilot training. He rents a bachelor pad at the swinging Chateaux Dijon in Houston, where he plays volleyball, drinks beer and dates. That year alone 6,065 American service people are killed in Vietnam.

"George Walker Bush is one member of the younger generation who doesn't get his kicks from pot or hashish or speed. He gets high all right, but not from narcotics."
—press release from the Texas Air National Guard

GW takes time off to join his father's second campaign for the US Senate. In the year of Kent State, Republican politics is not a big draw for youth. GW demonstrates his political pragmatism when recruiting interns, telling them they needn't believe in the party platform or even the candidate.

Despite GW's best efforts, Dad's Senate bid fails. Dad's consolation prize is to be appointed national head of the Republican Party. In this position he brings lofty Bush principles and Bush moral guidance to the GOP. Even though he's head of the party throughout, he remains unscathed by the Watergate scandals.

While running the RNC Daddy Bush also meets a talented young party operative just out of college, Karl Rove.

1972 — Perhaps pushed to the edge by his father's failed senate campaign and the relentless demands of weekend reserve duty (he has to report once or twice a month), GW, according to friends, spends weekdays chain-smoking, getting drunk, getting high on pot, and occasionally snorting coke.

1973 — GW's grounded from his Air National Guard service two years before the end of his tour of duty. He enrolls in Harvard Business School. His whereabouts for the last year of his Guard service are unknown. During GW's campaign for the presidency in 2000, Veterans groups will offer reward money to anyone who can account for his whereabouts during his last year in the military. The money will remain unclaimed.

1975 — GW graduates Harvard Business School. Sets off for Midland and the oil business with nothing but his Harvard MBA, a $100 a day job as a "land man" and a trust fund to sustain him.

1976 — GW arrested for drunk driving.

After his stint as Chair of the Republican National Committee and having guided the party through the shoals of Watergate, GW's Daddy is rewarded when Gerald Ford appoints him director of the CIA.

1977 — GW, in a move that would make Horatio Alger proud, starts his own oil drilling company—Arbusto Energy. In another one of life's strange coincidences one of his first investors turns out to be Philip Uzielli, an acquaintance of his Dad's and a close friend of Secretary of State James Baker.

Mutual friends match GW up with Laura Welch at a backyard barbecue. They are married later that year.

> *"[I found her to be] thoughtful, smart, interested . . . one of the great listeners. And since I'm one of the big talkers, it was a great fit."*
>
> —GW, on why it was love at first sight with Laura

1978 — Realizing he has a duty to spread his talents beyond the private sector, and convinced that Jimmy Carter is steering the US towards "European-style socialism," GW joins the Texas Republican primary race for Congress against ex-Odessa mayor Jim Reese. GW opposes the ERA as "unnecessary" and says he is against abortion personally but does not favor a "pro-life" amendment. He learns a lesson as his opponent out runs him on the right wing, slamming GW's Daddy for being a member of David Rockefeller's Trilateral Commission. The loss in the primary only whets GW's appetite for public service, but for now he must go back to the private sector.

1979 — GW raises "seed money" to organize a publicly registered drilling partnership in Midland. Surprisingly, financing again comes from the family. The money is provided by his Uncle Jonathan's clients. Drilling operations ensue.

1981 — Daddy Bush takes office as Vice President of the US. In Manila, the elder Bush engages in an early and awe inspiring act of "compassionate conservatism," admiringly toasting Ferdinand Marcos' "adherence to democratic principle" while generously overlooking Amnesty International's report that torture is "widespread and systematic" under his rule.

1984 — Perhaps bespeaking divine intervention to turn GW's path back toward public service, GW's Arbusto Energy goes bust. But there's always that "luck of the Bushes"—GW rescued from bankruptcy by Spectrum 7, which merges with his company.

1985 — Reverend Billy Graham plants "a mustard seed" in GW's soul, who begins thinking about God. "I know I'll never be perfect," he realizes.

1986 — GW's spiritual awakening. After a blowout 40th birthday bash, GW awakens the following morning in his hotel bathroom with matted hair, bloodshot eyes and vomit encrusted on his chin. He determines he is not "right with God." Begins to take Bible study classes.

Harken Energy purchases Spectrum 7. GW's biggest investor, Philip Uzielli, has lost nearly all the money he put in.

"Hard work, skillful investments, the ability to read an environment that was ever-changing and react quickly"
— GW on the secrets to his business success

1988 — GW's family values shine as he assumes the role of "hatchet man" for Daddy's presidential campaign. In an election that will be remembered for Bush's race-baiting Willie Horton attack ads, for which GW personally raises money, the Republicans revamp the "southern strategy" pioneered by Nixon, and Daddy Bush is elected 41st President of the United States.

1989 — GW's part of an effort to buy the Texas Rangers. He borrows half a million dollars from the United Bank of Midland to seal the deal and becomes managing general partner of the team. Duties are to attend a lot of baseball games.

"Folks see me sitting in the same seat they sit in, eating the same popcorn, peeing in the same urinal."
—GW on what his role in baseball meant to the common man

1990 — With more of that good old "luck of the Bushes" GW unloads 60% of his Harken energy stock — 212,140 shares, reaping a profit of $848,560, more than two-a-half-times the shares' original value. The transaction is miraculously completed a week before the end of a quarter in which the company posts loss of $23.2 million. When the result becomes public, the company stock declines to $2.37 a share. GW sold at $4.12 per share and denied insider knowledge—a feat of astounding self-discipline, since he sat on the board, the audit committee, and a panel looking into corporate restructuring.

GW and his Texas Rangers threaten to relocate the team unless the public funds a new stadium. GW uses political clout to get a bill passed creating quasi-governmental Arlington Sports Facility Development Authority. It seizes private land misusing powers of eminent domain and turns the condemned property over to the Rangers for future development. The Mathes family sues and ultimately wins for being forced to sell way below market value. GW makes a bundle and continues to tout his belief in the sanctity of private property.

1992 — Daddy is defeated by Bill Clinton. He and Mom need to vacate the White House. In a final burst of altruism and high-mindedness, Daddy issues pardons for his buddies caught arming terrorists and secretly selling missiles to Khomeini's Iran in the Iran-Contra scandal.

1993 — GW publicly declares that those who fail to accept Jesus Christ as their "personal savior" don't go to Heaven.

1994 — GW's life of sacrifice, delayed gratification, and hard work has paid off. He's the very image of the American dream, a Texas millionaire, whose path is clearly on the ascent.

"His insider-status investment of $500,000, which derived from his insider-status Harken stock, which derived from his insider status as a Bush son, eventually nets him a decent-sized fortune of $14 million."

—Journalist Michael Kelly

Having risked all to better the lives of Texans by providing them the joys of major league baseball, GW now turns his attention to further public service and, despite never having held any elected position, decides to run for governor of Texas. He rides a wave of reaction to defeat Anne Richards and win the governorship.

1995 — GW's faith in the free market is unbounded. A Public Citizen study reveals that three-fourths of the companies in which he owns stock are defendant corporations in what Bush likes to call frivolous lawsuits, including Baxter Trevanol Labs and Baxter International, companies embroiled in controversy over breast implant suits.

1996 — GW's policies as governor—deregulation, anemic social welfare, privatization, and stern intolerance, not to mention presiding over the busiest death row of any state in the nation cries out for a label. "Compassionate conservatism" is born.

1997 — GW's State of the State address unveils plan for complete overhaul of Texas' tax code. Demonstrating once again his loyalty to family values, particularly the value of his own family, GW pushes through $3 billion in tax cuts, mostly for the super rich.

1998 — Turnout soars to 32.5% as GW wins second term as Governor, outspending Democrat Garry Mauro four to one. "It's going to be somewhat difficult for the Republican Party to project a positive and optimistic national agenda until they get a candidate in the year 2000 who is positive and optimistic and conservative," GW tells reporter Wayne Slater. "Positive and optimistic" are adjectives GW often uses as a self-description.

1999 — Taking the "compassionate conservative" movement to its next level, GW opposes bill banning executions of retarded people, saying he likes the law "the way it is now." A study completed by the tri-national North American Commission on Environmental Cooperation determines that Texas pollutes more than any other state.

GW's abortion notification bill requires doctors to inform parents when their unmarried daughters (18 or younger) seek an abortion. No provision for daughters who fear their fathers will kill them.

Poll shows GW fares well because respondents think he is his father. GW makes light of the confusion: "In politics, an easily recalled name is a very, very important thing."

After one term as Governor, GW decides to reach yet higher and launches his bid for the presidency.

2000 — The Bush formula works again. Daddy's Rolodex, the family name, and $100 million or so from family and friends gets him the Republican nomination. GW is now positioned to avenge his father's loss to the Clintonites in the '92 election.

Sticking with the formula, GW selects one of Daddy's trusted lieutenants to help him pick a running mate.

With characteristic modesty Dick Cheney determines that the best man for the job is himself. The resulting GOP ticket is a perfect match made in the oilpatch, two Texas oil men (one from that part of Texas known for constitutional reasons, as Wyoming) sticking up for regular folks.

The two saddle up and head off to restore integrity to the presidency by expelling the selfish, indulgent, draft dodging, pot smoking, Clinton/Gore team from the White House. Drawing on oil-magnate-family- values that will emerge as the core of their administration, Bush and Cheney mount an aggressive attack, setting records for campaign cash raised and hammering away at the moral degradation and economic mismanagement of the Clinton/Gore Administration.

GW and Gore finish in practically a dead heat in the general election. Gore has actually won the popular vote by nearly half a million votes but in the electoral college the entire election comes down to Florida. In another stroke of Bush Luck Florida is run by GW's kid brother Jeb and the election is in the hands of Jeb's personal friend, Secretary of State Katherine Harris. In a month-long legal battle over the recount, Bush/Cheney bravely defend democracy and strive for a fair outcome. Unselfishly pouring $14 million into their efforts, they outspend Gore by 4 to 1 and use Enron's corporate jets to fly their squadrons of lawyers and political operatives around. No cost is too great in their quest to insure that justice is done.

At the last moment, with the Florida Supreme Court engaged in flagrant judicial activism designed to decide the outcome based on counting all the ballots, the US Supreme Court intervenes in the name of rationality and fairness and hands the election to Bush/Cheney.

2001 — GW is sworn in as the 43rd President of the United States— just another example of how an average white guy can make it to the top on nothing more than blue-blood connections, an ivy-league degree, a trust fund, and an ex-president for a father.

THE COLLECTED WISDOM OF GEORGE W. BUSH

GW On Himself

"You know, I could run for governor but I'm basically a media creation. I've never done anything. I've worked for my dad. I worked in the oil business. But that's not the kind of profile you have to have to get elected to public office."

—GW to good friend and Yale classmate Roland Betts, 1989

GW Ignores Marijuana and Cocaine Charges For Sake of Others
(and redefines childhood so that it runs into your early thirties….)

"I have made mistakes. I choose not to inventory my sins because I don't want anybody to be able to say, 'Well, the governor of Texas did it, why shouldn't I?' That's why I have been somewhat mysterious about my past . . . I'm not going to talk about what I did as a child. It is irrelevant what I did 20 to 30 years ago."

—GW on the presidential campaign trail

Ethics According To GW: If I Feel Good, I'm Telling The Truth

"I'm very comfortable in looking you in the eye and saying I did nothing wrong on this."

—GW to the press on his insider trading with Harken energy stock, adding that his stock sale was "entirely legal and proper"

GW On How To Handle A Setback

"If we lose this one, we're dead. Get out a dirty tricks book, Lee, and start reading."

—GW to Lee Atwater, after his Dad finished third in the Iowa caucuses in 1988

GW Justifies An Appointment To High Office

"Because he gave money to my father."

—GW, justifying proposing Dallas catalog baron Roger Horchow for chairman of the National Endowment for the Arts

GW Has Second Thoughts

"The double-crossing son-of-a-bitch. Cross his name off the list."

—GW, changing his mind about Horchow after discovering he had given money to both Daddy Bush and Michael Dukakis

GW Goes Modest

"I am humbled by the response. I am, as you well can imagine, amazed at the outpouring of support. This is a campaign that has got a wide range of people who are willing to help people from all around the country. I'm gratified and that's that."

—GW, after raising $37 million in the first six months of 1999, an all-time record—at the time

Sociable George

"I've got a lot of friends."

—GW, attempting to explain the mountain of wealth cascading into his campaign coffers

Relax, Someone Else is at the Helm… Not Just Dick Cheney…

"I could not [have been] governor if I did not believe in a divine plan that supersedes all human plans."

—GW quoted in *The Leadership Genius of George W. Bush*

And You Call Yourself A Republican?

"I try not to put people into categories and lump people into groups."

—GW Bush, as Governor of Texas

That's-More-Like-It Department

"You're either with us or you're with the terrorists."

—GW Bush, as President of the US

CHAPTER TWO

THE IMMACULATE SELECTION

HOW SCRUBBING THE VOTER ROLLS MADE FLORIDA'S 2000 ELECTIONS WHITER

Count Dollars, Not Ballots

"Before God, before my family, before my friends, before my nation, before the nation, I sleep well at night."
—Katherine Harris, 2002

I think all of us agree that the 2000 elections were a high point for American democracy. Once and for all we got rid of that detestable, one-person, one-vote standard that has been holding us back for so long. And as so many pundits sagely observed, docilely accepting the loser of the election as the winner proved the vibrancy and strength of our democracy.

It was, indeed, a triumph of the democratic spirit when Katherine Harris and Jeb Bush purged 57,700 "felons" from Florida voter registries. Granted, civilized sectors of the world have long abandoned the practice of depriving ex-convicts of their voting rights, and

yes, over 90% of those on the Florida lists were legally entitled to vote. But let's face it, denying these folks the vote and blocking another 40,000 people from registering should not prevent us from recognizing that the disenfranchised were primarily black and Latino, groups that have long had difficulty voting Republican. And how can we let people vote when they are biased like that?

Now, about the irregularities. Sure, 325 of the purged were listed as criminals on the basis of crimes committed in the future. But let's not knock clairvoyance until we've given it a chance. Same goes for the 4,000 names next to blank conviction dates. Until these people prove they haven't committed a crime sometime, somewhere, somehow, I don't think we can trust them with a vote. After all, if the President's brother has your name on a list, you must be guilty of something.

Oddly, some people make a big deal out of the fact that the blacklist was drawn up by DataBase Technologies, a division of Choice Point, which is loaded with Republican fat-cats, not that that's important. Others find it suspicious that Professional Service Inc. charged just $5,700 to make sure the voting rolls were shipshape in 1998, while DataBase Technology's fee in 2000 was $2,317,800 for the same job.

There's an easy explanation. See, the work DataBase Technologies did was inaccurate, unfinished, incompetent, and disastrous to democracy. That's why they were hired back and given another whopping fee. Professional Service Inc. just couldn't compete on this level. If things had been left up to them, we might have reverted to the discredited practice of encouraging turnout and counting the ballots. Now that's no way to run a democracy.

Anyway, not to worry. Everything was supervised with nonpartisan professionalism by Jeb Bush, who simply exudes integrity from every pore. That's why I see nothing amiss in Choice Point vice president James Lee admitting that Florida officials specifically asked that the names of innocent people be put on their blacklist. Nor do I find it odd that individuals were requested purged on the basis that the letters of their last name coincided with some of the letters in a known felon's last name. Obviously, programmed inaccuracy is needed to insure that the best man (i.e. richest) wins the election. For example, if Scott Peterson committed a crime, Scott Peters has to lose his vote too. And Peter Scott. And Scott Petersen. And a guy named

Peterson or Peters with the nickname "Scout." And Scott Patterson, too, for that matter.

By the way, I think we should be grateful that Florida is one of the few states that includes both party affiliation and race on its registration files, which insured that purged Florida voters were overwhelmingly members of the Republican-hating races. And thank God Florida never counted 179,855 ballots at all. A lot of people got bent out of shape about that, especially after they learned that the "spoiled" vote ratio registered much higher in counties with a lot of blacks than in overwhelmingly white counties. But there's another easy answer to that: Get over it.

Anyway, who really cares how many votes a candidate gets? What counts is dollars, not ballots. And with King George gunning to raise a couple hundred million dollars for 2004, what's the point of counting ballots at all?

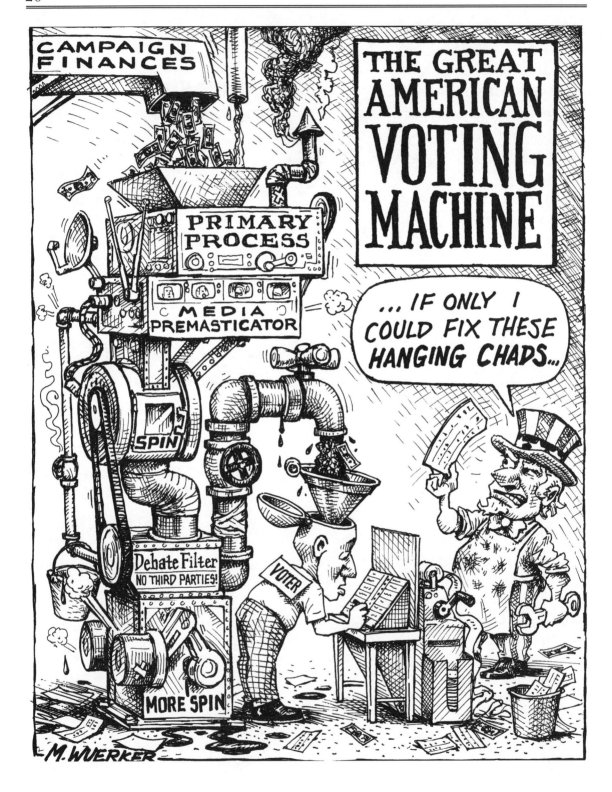

POST TRAUMATIC ELECTION SYNDROME

AND IT'S MANY MANIFESTATIONS...

C.N.N.-SOMNIA
(too many pontificating pundits)

LIMBAUGHTIMAZATION
(too much Talk Radio)

HYPERLEGALALYSIS
(too many court decisions)

DEPRESSED CHADS
(too many "Chad" jokes)

M. WUERKER

TRUTH IN ADVERTISING

What the Republican campaign slogans should be in the 2004 Election...

Pity The Rich

Don't Conserve - Stripmine!

No Wage Too Low . . . No Air Too Dirty . . . No Lie Too Big ...Vote Republican

Shed Those Unwanted 401(k)s

Spread Your Legs - Go To Jail

Make Rubble, Not Jobs

Abolish The Environment

Torture Evildoers

WorldCom, Yes! Medicare, No!

Tests, Not Teachers

Americanize Islam Now!

Only Evildoers Demand Rights

"Old South" Good,
"Old Europe" Bad

Another American For Secret
Tribunals

Dump "Rights," Not Ashcroft

Support Our Chickenhawks

Thanks For Exploiting Our 9-11
Grief

Jails, Not Jobs

Bin Laden: Smoke Him Out
and Forget Him

Arrest Debate, Not Bin Laden

Spy On Me: I'm Dangerous

Enronize My Pension Now!

The Crusades - Not Just For
The Middle Ages Anymore

From our button collection:

Invade Iraq	Invade Turkey
Invade Iran	Invade Colombia
Invade Syria	Invade Venezuela
Invade Egypt	Invade Peru
Invade Libya	Invade Argentina
Invade Saudi Arabia	Invade Ecuador
Invade the Philippines	Invade France
Invade North Korea	Invade Cuba

CHAPTER THREE

THE ARSONISTS RUNNING THE FIRE DEPARTMENT

THE COMMITTEE TO RE-SELECT THE PRESIDENT

M.WUERKER

VICE-PRESIDENT

MAKING AMERICAN CAPITALISM WORK FOR YOU:
WHY WE LOVE "BIG DICK"

General Background: Oil executive, member of the White House staff (1975-77), Wyoming Representative (1979-89), Defense Secretary (1989-1993), CEO Halliburton Oil, (1995-1999).

As a Congressman Cheney was the Strom Thurmond of the West, voting against:

* the Equal Rights Amendment
* funding for Head Start
* a resolution calling for South Africa to release Nelson Mandela from prison
* federal funding for abortion even in cases of rape or incest
* a ban on cop killer bullets
* restrictions on plastic guns that could easily be slipped through airport security
* safe drinking water standards
* establishing the federal Department of Education
* a waiting period for handgun purchases
* the Panama Canal Treaty
* against imposing sanctions on apartheid South Africa (but only 10 times).

When pressed, he indicated that budget pressures induced many of these votes, which is quite plausible. There's no telling how much it would have cost to release Mandela from prison.

PUBLIC SERVANT

Defense Secretary under Papa Bush, Cheney led US forces in two slaughters, excuse me, military operations, the invasion of Panama, which restored the traditional white, European elite to power, and the first Gulf War, which restored the Kuwaiti monarchy. According to the Panamanian Human Rights Commission, US troops killed between two and three thousand civilians in Panama, while in the Gulf War Pentagon officials estimate 200,000 Iraqis were killed.

While Cheney was still at the Pentagon, the DoD commissioned a Halliburton subsidiary—Brown & Root—to do a classified study on whether it was advisable to contract out more military work to the private sector. The surprising answer was yes and over the next eight years Brown & Root and another company were awarded 2,700 federal contracts, not that the two events are related at all.

GOOD CORPORATE CITIZEN

Meanwhile Dick Cheney—a man with zero business experience— became CEO of Halliburton two years after leaving the government, nearly doubling the value of the company's federal contracts while becoming deliriously rich himself. Charles Lewis of the Center for Public Integrity explains the incest-is-best relation that makes such happy outcomes possible: "They [military officials] have classified clearances; they go to classified meetings; and they're with companies getting billions of dollars in classified contracts; and their disclosures about their activities are classified." What could be fairer?

"You've got to go where the oil is."
—Dick Cheney, 1998

Human rights abuses are no obstacle to Cheney's profiteering, thank God. When Halliburton got to help rebuild Iraq's petroleum industry after Cheney and Co. destroyed it in the first Gulf War, Big Dick expressed no reservations about profiting off relations with Evil Incarnate, Saddam Hussein. Nor did he have any objection to Halliburton working with the repressive government of Burma or with Chevron and Shell in Nigeria, another country with light smudges on its human rights record. At the same time, leaders like Equatorial Guinea's Obiang Nguema Mbasogo and Congo President Denis Sassou-Nguesso were enriching themselves and their families with the revenues provided by Halliburton-built offshore oil platforms while brutally crushing their political opposition. Not that there's anything wrong with that.

As soon as US forces took over Baghdad in 2003, a familiar team won out again as tens of billions of dollars worth of government contracts were awarded based on secret bidding arrangements. Halliburton subsidiary Brown & Root was selected to put out oil fires and handle other duties involving damage to Iraq's oil industry. Cheney's relation to the company was purely coincidental.

Back in the mid-1990s, Cheney had rolled up his sleeves and generously helped the company avoid tax liability. During his term as CEO, Halliburton created dozens of dummy offices in offshore tax havens in the Cayman Islands. The number of Halliburton subsidiaries registered in tax havens went from 9 to 44 in the five years Cheney was at the helm. Halliburton's federal taxes dropped from $302 million in 1998 to a negative $85 million, that is, the company got an $85 million rebate in 1999. At the same time Halliburton received $2.3 billion in government contracts and $1.5 billion in government financing and loan guarantees. During his vice-presidential debate with Joe Lieberman in 2000, Cheney insisted that the government had had "absolutely nothing to do" with Halliburton's financial success. $3.8 billion = 0. It must be that new math.

GOOD CORPORATE GOVERNANCE

During a fund-raising appearance in the summer of 2002 Cheney tried his hand at stand-up comedy, praising the White House's commitment to "more accountability for corporate officials." Of course, when he was at Halliburton, the company had charged the Pentagon $750,000 for work that actually cost them $125,000. Hilarious, isn't it?

Another career highlight for Cheney occurred when California spun into financial disaster from a phony energy crisis arranged by Enron. Cheney had six meetings with Enron representatives, including two with CEO Ken Lay, the last just six days prior to the company's revelation that it had vastly overstated its earnings. While Enron executives cashed out over $1 billion in company stock before the day of reckoning, their employees lost their pensions and their jobs— just in time for the Christmas season. Cheney had nothing to do with it, of course.

When he left Halliburton, Cheney received $13 million in severance pay and left behind millions of dollars in losses from bad investments, a spate of SEC investigations, and a pile of lawsuits, not that there's anything wrong with that. The value of Halliburton stock plunged.

Cheney returned to comedy mode after the Bush Administration abandoned its campaign promise to regulate carbon dioxide emissions. Big Dick said the promise had been a mistake because carbon dioxide isn't a pollutant. David Doniger of the Natural Resources Defense Council commented: "If carbon dioxide isn't a pollutant, maybe ketchup is a vegetable after all." With a little work, he may be as funny as Cheney some day.

GOOD PLANETARY STEWARDSHIP

Ecology is perhaps Cheney's strongest suit. When he was faced with a series of potentially ruinous asbestos-related lawsuits at Halliburton, the company decided it should

lobby for a change of law rather than argue the cases in court. So Cheney and his company shelled out nearly half a million dollars to congressional candidates between 1997 and 2000, with $157,000 directed to 62 lawmakers who found it in their hearts to co-sponsor bills limiting the liability of asbestos manufacturers. Democracy in action!

Cheney is a big fan of drilling for oil in the Arctic National Wildlife Reserve, which can supply US energy needs for weeks on end. On the other hand, his Energy Task Force killed a plan to increase fuel-efficiency standards, which would have saved 2.5 million barrels of oil a day—permanently.

Like all Republicans, Cheney cherishes family values, which is why at the 2000 Republican Convention in Philadelphia he would not appear on the victory platform with his lesbian daughter.

Of course, she's merely kin. His real family is Halliburton, Enron, Philip Morris, AT&T, Microsoft, and the Pentagon.

A PATTERN EMERGES...

M.WUERKER

DONALD RUMSFELD

"RUMMY" SPELLS REFRESHMENT

Former Drug Company Executive, US Representative from Illinois (1963-69), Assistant to the President (1969-75), Secretary of Defense (1975-77), President GD Searle (1977-85). His heart is owned by G. D. Searle, Tribune Company, Motorola, Gulfstream Aerospace, General Dynamics, Sears Roebuck, Allstate, and Kellogg.

Henry Kissinger rates him the most ruthless man he has ever known, which is certainly high praise coming from the guy who carpet bombed three Southeast Asian countries to vast and lifeless moonscapes.

A hawk's hawk, Rumsfeld is with the Wolfowitz-Cheney-Perle school of diplomacy, which posits world-wide US hegemony as a prerequisite to the moral advancement of the human race. He is also closely linked to Frank Gaffney's Center for Security Policy, which is command central of the Star Wars lobby. Their grand idea is to plant lasers in the heavens and usher in world peace. I can hardly wait.

Rummy serves on the board of Empower America, as does William Bennett, who once endorsed beheading drug traffickers, and Jeane Kirkpatrick, who found Washington's death squad governments during the Cold War merely "moderately authoritarian," as opposed to the "totalitarian" (i.e. really really bad) Communist world.

In 1998 Rumsfeld predicted that the US would be threatened by North Korean missiles within five years, a remarkably accurate forecast helped to fulfillment by King George's calling Kim Jong Il a "pygmy" and slamming North Korea for being part of an "Axis of Evil." For some reason, the North Koreans took offense at this and then concluded from the liberation of Iraq that the Bush Administration is in the imperialism business. This is preposterous, of course, it's not like we've seized anyone's oil or anything, but you know how those Commies love anti-capitalist rhetoric!

Earth is entirely too small to contain Rummy's impressive foreign policy ambitions. Not long before his appointment as Secretary of Defense, he headed a Pentagon commission warning that America might soon face a "space Pearl Harbor." The commission's report argued for tighter security for US space systems and the appointment of an undersecretary of defense for space, intelligence, and information, going on to state that the president should "have an option to deploy weapons in space to deter threats to, and, if necessary, defend against attacks on US interests." Many people still don't know this, but Al Qaeda has recruited martian

YOUR GUIDE TO Moral Wafare

Moral Missile

Immoral Missile

Moral Munition Delivery System

Immoral Munition Delivery System

Morally Justifiable Collateral Damage

Morally Unjustifiable Collateral Damage

sleeper cells throughout the universe to unleash inter-galactic strikes at us. This makes it imperative that we do whatever Rummy tells us to.

Like the rest of his fellow members of the Project for the New American Century, Rumsfeld argues persuasively that arms control is counterproductive. The problem is that deterrence depends on the willingness to wage war, but arms control is based on a fear of going to war, which you shouldn't admit you have because it undermines deterrence. Plus, once you enter into arms limitation agreements there's a disturbing tendency to curb arms production. If this happens, there is much less opportunity to achieve and extend advantages over adversaries, which, once again, undermines deterrence. There is absolutely no end to this terrifying process, which could, in a worst-case scenario, actually bring about —God forbid— peace! Try not to think about it.

After the US renounced support for the Rome Treaty establishing the International Criminal Court, Rumsfeld weighed in with the observation that the ICC would "necessarily complicate US military cooperation," adding that an international court with jurisdiction over genocide, war crimes, and crimes against humanity "could well create a powerful disincentive for US military engagement in the world." Horrors! Another threat of peace. Fortunately, Rummy refused to recognize that that was exactly what the treaty was for and that much of the world sees little distinction between US "military engagement" and war crimes.

We are so unappreciated these days.

SECRETARY OF STATE COLIN POWELL

EQUAL IN WAR CRIMES

As an Army officer in Vietnam Powell pierced the lily-white enclave of war criminals, helping cover up atrocities by troops from the same brigade that perpetrated the My Lai Massacre.

An admirer of Dr. King, Powell reached out a helping hand to blood-soaked Ayatollahs in need during the Reagan years, supervising the army's transfer of 4,508 TOW missiles to the CIA, nearly half of which were destined for Iran.

Warning Central American states of a cut-off in US aid if support were not extended to Contra mercenaries killing thousands of Nicaraguans infected with social justice ambitions, Powell bravely defended against the deadly threat of Sandinista schools, health clinics, and agricultural coops sweeping up the Rio Grande in the 1980s. He was also the key player in Papa Bush's 1989 effort to "kick a little ass" in Panama, an invasion that killed thousands of residents of Panama City in the effort to capture a single ex-CIA thug. Talk about military efficiency!

Combining business with pleasure, Powell gloated over the U.S. destruction of two live nuclear reactors during Gulf War I: "The two operating reactors they had are both gone, they're down, they're finished." When asked for the number of Iraqis killed in the war, he said, "It's really not a number I'm terribly interested in." Next time someone asks you how many Jews died in the Holocaust, try that answer out. It's a real howler!

In 1993, after the UN Truth Commission published its report naming top Salvadoran officers involved in the assassination of six Jesuits and their housekeeper, Powell paid a thoughtful visit to El Salvador and congratulated the armed forces. Here's a guy who knows it's good for morale to pat the men on the back once in a while.

In 2000, while thousands of blacks were being fraudulently deprived of the vote in Florida, Powell went to Crawford, Texas to pose for a photo-op in support of Bush's presidential bid. In February 2001, Powell announced his determination to "reenergize" the sanctions against Iraq that had barely killed a million people at that point. He was proud after the US diverted public attention from the dying Iraqis. "We have succeeded, because we stopped the talking about Iraqi children, and instead are talking about weapons of mass destruction, not sanctions to hurt civilians."

While Israel went on a massive West Bank killing spree in the Spring of 2002, Powell dawdled in Morocco, Spain, Jordan, and Egypt, giving Sharon the chance to bury people alive in Jenin. Diplomacy in action!

After the US killed thousands of Iraqi civilians in its 2003 invasion, Powell told the *LA Times* that the next of kin were sure to see the best in Washington: "The people of Iraq will have confidence in us because of who we are and what we've done."

Now that's a role model!

SPIN MISTRESS EXTRAORDINAIRE

She sees other countries as unimportant, finding Israel's problem to be that it is "so small" while pitiful Cuba is merely "the road kill of history."

A former director of Charles Schwab and Transamerica, she has served as an adviser for JP Morgan and had a 130,000 ton oil tanker named after her for being a member of Chevron's board of directors. Impressed by the petroleum industry's ecological wisdom, she says, "Oil companies have come a long way in their environmental policies . . . They are good citizens." Right!

Of course, there was that lawsuit charging Chevron with aiding Nigeria's military police in smashing public demonstrations against the company's exploitation of the Nigerian delta, but that's no big deal. Well, OK, a Chevron oil tanker with 35,000 tons of fuel did run aground off the coast of Denmark in February 2003, just a few months after another tanker sank off the coast

of Spain, spilling one-third of its 77,000 tons of fuel oil and causing an environmental disaster. And, yes, there was a 1999 Chevron explosion in Richmond, California which sent 600 people to the hospital while firefighters battled for five hours to contain the resulting toxic blaze. But at least nothing serious happened.

OK, sure, BP Amoco did spill 9,700 gallons of oil in Prudhoe Bay, Alaska in 2001, six years after being convicted of illegally dumping hazardous waste in nearby groundwater. And Exxon was accused by the EPA of almost 200 violations of the Clean Air Act in 1998 alone, but hey, let's not get picky; after all, bad things happen to good companies. And it's true that over the past quarter century there have been about three dozen spills, leaks, blowouts, or illegal discharges from Chevron oil fields, drilling rigs, or pipelines, while in the decade 1991-2001 the "Dirty Four" of British Petroleum, ExxonMobil, Chevron, and Phillips Petroleum treated us to more than 150 spills (thanks guys!). And it's also a fact that these four oil giants have over 100 Superfund toxic waste sites and have caused over 40 deaths in explosions and accidents in recent years. But the point is that it's a whole new day now and the oil companies are run by bio-diversity enthusiasts, so cancel Earth Day, disband the EPA, and abolish Greenpeace.

In addition to her charming notion of green oil companies, Rice also has a refreshingly innovative approach to remedying the legacy of slavery— forget about it! In September 2001, the US walked out of the World Conference Against Racism in Durban, South Africa because of horrifying plans to discuss "just and adequate reparation . . . to redress acts of racism, racial discrimination, xenophobia and related intolerance." Condoleezza sensibly remarked that the pursuit of civilized life requires that we forget the past. Sounds good to me. Adolf Hitler? Who's he? Holocaust-schmolocaust, never heard of it—get a life!

On May 16, 2002, Rice showed just why she is the best person to serve as National Security Advisor, saying: "I don't think anybody could have predicted that these people would take an airplane and slam it into the World Trade Center, take another one and slam it into the Pentagon; that they would try to use an airplane as a missile." Of course, Tom Clancy wrote about just such possibilities in *Debt of Honor*, while former deputy director of the CIA John Gannon in a September 1999 National Intelligence Council report warned that, "Suicide bomber(s) belonging to al-Qaeda's Martyrdom Battalion could crash-land an aircraft packed with high explosives (C-4 and Semtex) into the Pentagon, the headquarters of the Central Intelligence Agency (CIA), or the White House." But hey, that's just a bunch of vague "chatter" that no one can make any sense of.

A principled advocate of Ari Fleischer's "watch what you say" doctrine, Rice met with television network executives to make sure they didn't air any speeches by Osama Bin Laden during the Afghanistan war. Ari characterized the talks as "collegial." It's so nice to see the state working hand in glove with the media like that.

DEPUTY UNDERSECRETARY OF DEFENSE

PAUL WOLFOWITZ "THE WOLF" THINKS LIKE A FOX

Number two man at the Pentagon, he is part of a group of empire builders that calls itself the Vulcans after the God of Fire. Among his insights is that the US bears no responsibility for injustice in the world.

In a brilliant deduction he once figured out that Communist expansionism was the cause of the Vietnam War, anti-colonial revolts in Africa, the anti-apartheid movement, and anti-dictatorship uprisings in Central America and Indonesia. With the Red Menace thus lapping at the American heartland he had no other choice but to help engineer a 50% real increase in US military spending in the Reagan years, which had nothing to do with the steady decline in American living standards that immediately followed and has continued ever since.

M. WUERKER

The freest of free thinkers, Wolfowitz opposes nuclear test bans and the anti-ballistic missile treaty, in fact, all diplomatic options restricting US dominance, because only dominance can bring us peace on our terms. His refreshing approach to arms control is to insist that the world submit to US demands, which is simply a stunning innovation in international relations. His preferred method of defense is to build a Star Wars shield whose purpose is "protecting a missile with a missile so it can destroy a missile," in the words of anti-nuclear activist Dr. Helen Caldicott. The fact that it encourages a worldwide nuclear arms race is a small price to pay for safety.

A man of the world, Wolfowitz was US Ambassador to Jakarta from 1986 to 1989. He was also a member of the US-Indonesia Society, a private group funded by American investors and long linked to the jolly folks in Indonesian intelligence and the military.

In May 1997, the Wolf informed Congress of "significant progress [in human rights] that Indonesia has already made," much of which was owed "to the strong and remarkable leadership of President Suharto." Remarkable indeed. Suharto is what economist Edward Herman calls a "good genocidist." With Washington's full support he exterminated an estimated 500,000 to a million-plus of his own people, subsequently invading East Timor and massacring 200,000 more, the largest liquidation relative to population size since the Holocaust.

But it was all for a good cause— defense of Indonesia's "investor's paradise." A low-wage, high-repression region like that is worth an ocean of blood, which is why Wolfowitz has such fond memories of dear General Suharto.

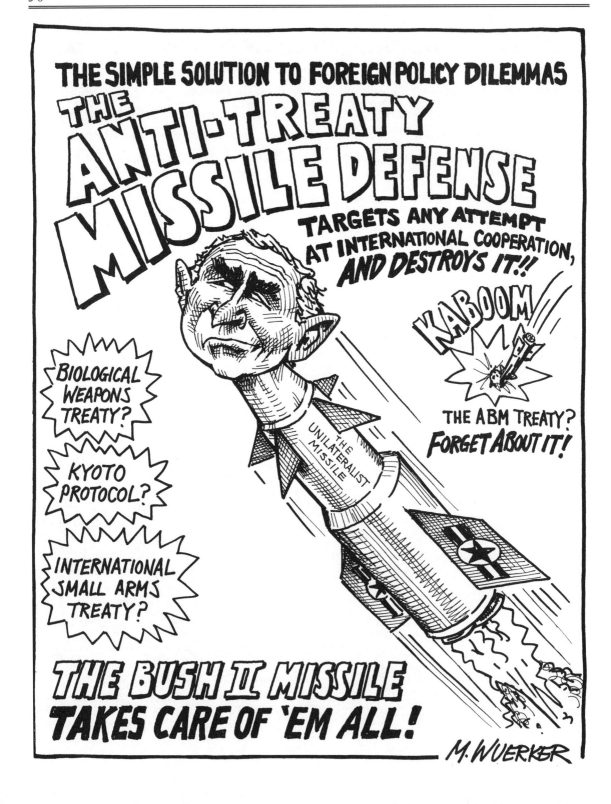

THE PRINCE OF DARKNESS*

A Senate aide who had known him for a decade by the beginning of the Reagan years said he had a split personality: "There's a very courtly . . . very ingratiating, very charming sort of person . . . There's another side; it is dark . . . his face itself literally becomes dark . . . it's a very intense, humorless, compulsive personality that will not let go." Hence his nickname the "Prince of Darkness."

"He's extremely vindictive and narrow-minded," said Dimitri Simes, onetime executive director of the Soviet and East European research program at Johns Hopkins University. Robert Gordon, a Massachusetts businessman who knew him through work on behalf of Soviet Jewry described him as "a very tough guy [who] is willing to bring up any kind of dirt that might change your opinion of someone." Vindictive, narrow-minded, and prone to smear anyone in his way—a true public servant.

On policy matters, Perle has long advocated unrestrained US weapons production and the tearing up of arms control treaties. During the Nuclear Freeze era he was with the crowd that thought a nuclear war could be "won." In 1983, he declared that the prospect of nuclear winter wiping out all life on earth was "all the more reason to continue President Reagan's weapons buildup." Right. Deterrence can't work if you freak out about the details of nuclear war.

A good deal of Perle's career has been spent promoting the anti-Communist theology that kept morgues hopping throughout the world. He regarded the USSR as "another Hitler's Germany," a judgment confirmed by events when hordes of emaciated prisoners streamed out of Soviet death camps in 1991. Who can ever forget them?

A hard-line Israel supremacist, Perle is also a member of the Project for the New American Century , which favors a US take-over of the Middle East and permanent American domination of the world. He is delighted with the "death" of the UN, which he regards as an irrelevant "chatterbox on the Hudson," devoted to ludicrous fantasies of effective international law.

Perle argued for regime change in Iraq on the grounds that Saddam Hussein was a thoroughly bad man, which no one had ever realized before. He dismissed weapons inspections on the grounds that absence of evidence is not evidence of absence: "All he [weapons inspector Hans Blix] can know is the results of his own investigations. And that does not prove Saddam does not have weapons of mass destruction." So don't jump to conclusions. Just because two plus two equals four does not prove it doesn't equal five, right?

Let's follow Richard's lead and keep an open mind about things.

* what his friends actually call him—really.

SENIOR ADVISER TO THE PRESIDENT KARL ROVE

CAPTAIN SMEAR

"The man's got no soul."

—Ed Wendler, a Democratic consultant who met Rove in his early career

---

"I have no other persona than Bush."
—Karl Rove, 2000

A lifelong admirer of Richard Nixon and a colleague of the late Lee Atwater, he learned the delightful art of smearing early on and taught "dirty tricks" as chairman of the College Republicans National Committee.

In the 2000 presidential race he showed off his talent by destroying John McCain, a man who was tortured so extensively by Hanoi that he still walked with a limp 30 years later and couldn't lift his arms high enough to comb his hair. Rumors were spread that the torture had left him mentally unstable, that he was gay, that he had fathered an illegitimate child with a North Vietnamese woman, that he had a black daughter, that he had voted for the largest tax increase ever, that his wife had stolen prescription drugs from a charity and abused them while she was supposedly caring for their four kids, that McCain was pro-abortion, that he had abandoned his crippled first wife, and that he was a liar, a cheat, and a fraud. This happened the same year Rove said that, "People are more attracted today by a positive agenda than by wedge issues."

Rove is a firm believer that the 1960s are a permanent blight on the national record. His Bible on the decade is Myron Magnet's book, *The Dream and the Nightmare: The Sixties Legacy to the Underclass*, which he hands out like candy. Its thesis is that lazy minds like Bill Clinton transmitted their repulsive notions of free love and self-fulfillment to the poor, thus incapacitating them for lifting themselves out of poverty by hard work and self-discipline. That's how Bush got to the top, isn't it?

Not one to get hung up on consistency, Rove avoided service in Vietnam but loves Teddy Roosevelt, who celebrated the martial virtues above all others.

According to wife Darby, Karl "has hundreds of friends and no one he's intimate with," which is certainly a novel form of friendship. I guess that makes him part of the great American tradition of inventors!

ATTENTION DEFICIT DISORDER

Americans find it hard to stay focused. We're the channel surfing, multi-tasking; Nintendoing distraction capital of the world. And when it comes to following the news we may suffer from the same inability to keep track of too many things at once. Fortunately for us we have media handlers who help us decide what it is we should be thinking about. They're our guides through the complex jungle of ideas and images that keep us on the right paths and not thinking about those things we shouldn't. It used to be, in the bad old days, journalism was left to journalists. Newsrooms were run by newsmen and reporting was done by reporters. These days though we have media professionals who help the news media of the nation do their jobs. Many of these professionals work as managers for the big corporations that now own much of our media. Companies like General Electric, Disney, AOL make sure that many of their smartest people are managing our news for us. Some of these professionals have experience in government and even know many of our political leaders. Roger Ailes, the chairman of Fox News Network now works for a nice billionaire from Australia named Rupert Murdoch. Before that he ran the campaign that got George HW Bush elected president, as well as working as a media guru for the campaigns of Richard Nixon and Ronald Reagan. He's now hard at work bringing us the news that's "fair and balanced" on the fastest growing cable news network.

We also have people in the government working hard to manage what it is we talk about in the news. Some people put them down as spin-doctors but really they're just like any other doctor—concerned for our well being and helping us deal with our "attention deficit disorder." Karl Rove is one of the best at helping us with our focus. As Bush's political director (going back to his first failed attempts to run for congress), Dr. Karl has been very adept at keeping America's "eye on the ball" especially when it comes to scrutinizing George W. Bush.

AFTER THE SUCCESS OF HIS "TOP GUN" PHOTO SHOOT ON THE AIRCRAFT CARRIER GEORGE BUSH MIGHT CONDIDER SOME OTHER "COSTUME OPS"

"THE CORE"

"IT TAKES A THIEF"

"THE HULK"

During the 2000 campaign he kept the focus on the questionable integrity of Bill Clinton and his side-kick Al Gore. American was ready to "restore integriy to the White House" and Dr. Rove made it clear that GW Bush was just the draft-dodging, frat house, drunk driving, party boy to do it.

During the mid-term elections of 2002, Dr. Rove made sure that we stayed focused on the threat that Iraq posed to our nation. The daily drumbeat of threats and revelations of possible weapons of mass destruction from the evil dictator Saddam Hussein kept us from discussing or thinking about distracting things. Things like massive corporate scandals, several of which had uncomfortably close ties to figures in the administration, the swan dive in the equity markets, rising unemployment and the return in two short years to mas-

sive federal deficits. But the media strategy of the White House kept us focused on the threat from the madman on the other side of the world, Saddam that is, Osama Bin Laden (and the failure to find him) had by this time become a danger-ous distraction as well, one that Rove also worked hard to keep from disrupting the more important agenda.

JOHN ASHCROFT - "BIG ASH"

Attorney General of Missouri, 1976-1985, Governor of Missouri, 1985-1993, Senator from Missouri, 1994-2000. His heart belongs to AT&T, Microsoft, Monsanto, Enterprise Rent-A-Car, and Jefferson Davis.

"God's precious gift of life must be protected in law and nurtured in love."

— John Ashcroft

Closely tied to Pat Robertson, he is anti-tax, anti-abortion, anti-gambling, anti-National Endowment for the Arts, and anti-gay. He is for the death penalty, God, the Bible, and guns.

He voted against handgun control thirteen straight times, including votes against child safety locks, which are an obvious infringement of toddler liberty. Shortly after becoming Attorney General he announced that within 24-hours of purchase and background check, all background check files would be destroyed on gun buyers. So if you're into privacy, stock up on guns, which I'm sure Al Qaeda sleeper cells have already done.

As a policy-wonk, Ashcroft simply overflows with wisdom. He opposes legislation protecting gays against arbitrary firing. He is against abortion even in cases of rape or incest

---

"To those who scare peace loving people with phantoms of lost liberty, my message is this; your tactics only aid the terrorists..."
—Attorney General John Ashcroft 12/6/2001

---

or when the mother's life is endangered by the pregnancy. He is a big fan of the Drug War, which has made the US number one in the world at jailing non-violent people. He equates the defense of civil liberties with treason, which certainly sounds reasonable.

Ashcroft once gave the commencement address at Bob Jones University and has praised a neo-Confederate journal endorsing white separatism, apartheid, David Duke, and slavery. In 2000 he ran against Democratic Governor Mel Carnahan for a Missouri Senate seat. Just before the election Carnahan died in a plane crash.

Carnahan defeated Ashcroft.

DIRECTOR OF HOMELAND SECURITY

A RIDGE FOR THE LEMMINGS

The right-wing Commonwealth Foundation once praised him as "the most pro-business and pro-economic growth reformer in recent Pennsylvania history." As governor of the state he reduced inheritance taxes, deregulated electricity, cut worker's compensation, slashed welfare rolls, and jammed the jails with blacks and Latinos. For good meas-

"Pretty rational behavior."
    —Tom Ridge, on the purchase of duct tape as a defense against WMD

ure he proposed a pilot vouchers program to subsidize private and religious education and made Pennsylvania the largest importer of toxic waste in the country. Cancer enthusiasts were overjoyed.

Ridge was also a key architect and advocate of the beloved "Contract With America," which imposed fiscal austerity and the death penalty on the poor while sanctioning limit-less consumption for the rich. "Get tough" Ridge signed 214 death warrants in six years before achieving worldwide fame as the Duct Tape Czar. In this role he insists that the thoughts, words, and deeds of all Americans be instantly accessible to the political police as they battle evildoers for the soul of America.

When might the Bill of Rights be restored? "I don't think we'll ever be out of business," says Tom.

YOUR DEPARTMENT OF HOMELAND SECURITY'S RESPONSE TO OUR NEWLY HEIGHTENED TERROR ALERT...

PRAISE THE LORD! AND PASS THE DUCT TAPE!

SECRETARY OF THE INTERIOR

ECO-PRINCESS GAIL NORTON

A disciple of James Watt and a dear friend of the mining, logging, chemical and coal industries, she started her legal career with the Watt-founded Mountain States Legal Foundation. Later she became the associate solicitor at the Department of the Interior, where she worked to develop legal justification for drilling in the Arctic National Wildlife Refuge, which was pretty much a snap since the preserve has always been badly in need of oil derricks.

Norton is refreshingly enlightened on all social and environmental matters. She believes self-regulation by industry is the best approach to environmental protection and says property rights

include a "right to pollute." She has abetted strip mining in the Rocky Mountains and undermined wetlands protection. She has declared the Endangered Species Act unconstitutional. As Colorado's Attorney General in the mid-1990s she declined to press charges after a Gold Mine spilled cyanide into a local river, killing off all marine life along a 17 - mile stretch.

Also while A.G. in Colorado she gave a 1996 speech to the Independence Institue in which she equated slavery with "bad facts." She claimed that the embarrassing fact of slavery clouded an otherwise sound argument for states rights. She then offered the instructive analogy of her Colorado attorneys being forced to argue against intrusive federal auto emissions standards one luckless day when Denver was shrouded in severe smog.

Contrary to what many liberals claim, Norton isn't endorsing slavery with these remarks. She's merely comparing it to a SMOGGY DAY.

In the two years before joining the Bush Administration she was a lobbyist for the lead paint manufacturer, NL Industries, a defendant in suits involving 75 Superfund or other toxic waste sites. This company is also embroiled in lawsuits brought by families whose children are suffering lead-poisoning. In old tenement buildings, lead paint plaster flakes off the walls, ending up in the mouths of babies, who love its sweet taste. Some of them go blind or suffer brain damage as a result. Lawyers like Norton make sure NL Industries is well-defended against these greedy tykes, who are just looking for a hand out.

Anyway, according to the Centers For Disease Control, only one in 20 American kids suffers subclinical lead poisoning and most of them are children of color who just don't matter much in the grand political scheme of things. Many of them live in condemned housing owned by slumlords who evade the laws, which is a cinch since many of them are written with the generous help of the lead industry.

But hey, let's not get sentimental. This is capitalism, after all, so the priority is healthy profits and sick kids, not the other way around. Thanks Gail, for keeping things running this way!

SPECIAL ASSISTANT TO THE PRESIDENT AND SENIOR DIRECTOR FOR NEAR EAST AND NORTH AFRICA AFFAIRS

ELLIOT ABRAMS
DEAN OF DOUBLETHINK

"Death Squad" sounds so harsh... Let's call them "unlawful and arbitrary deprivation of life" squads

He's Baaaaaaaaaaack!

It's so nice to see old friends like Elliot back in government work. As Assistant Secretary of State for Human Rights under Ronald Reagan, he rated US counter-insurgency operations in El Salvador a "fabulous achievement," which nobody can deny. Seventy thousand Salvadorans were wiped out by US-backed security forces in a decade-and-a-half of strenuous merriment. Elliot was characteristically modest in declining to take full credit on Washington's behalf. When the US-trained Atlacatl battalion beheaded two hundred men in Church in the El Mozote Massacre, he bashfully attributed the deed to "Communist propaganda."

He was also the point man in the State Department's effort to clear up the ambiguity in the word murder, which failed to distinguish good killing from bad killing. As he explained: "We found the term 'killing' too broad and have substituted the more precise, if more verbose 'unlawful or arbitrary deprivation of life.'" More precise and more verbose. Nice!

Elliot admitted lying to Congress about the Iran-Contra scandal, but only because "he wasn't authorized to tell the truth." Explaining the matter by letter to Claiborne Pell, Chairman of the Senate Foreign Relations Committee, he wrote: "I regret that my October statements to the Congress on this subject—which I believed to be absolutely true—proved to be inaccurate." Now there's a run of bad luck for you! How could he have known at the time that his bald face lies would later "prove to be inaccurate?"

Many found his remarks quite moving. For example, Missouri Senator Thomas Eagleton (D), who told Elliot after hearing his testimony: "I want to puke."

Throughout the 1980s, Elliot worked diligently to destroy the Sandinista revolution in Nicaragua, objecting to priorities like land to the landless, food to the hungry, medical aid to the sick. Yuck! Abrams promised a happy ending to the proxy war, which was carried out mostly by ex-Somoza National Guardsmen famous for torture, rape, and murder. Said Abrams: "When history is written, the contras will be folk heroes." I certainly hope so!

At the same time, tens of thousands of Indians were being helped into the afterlife by Washington's client state in neighboring Guatemala. Elliot discounted reports of mass killings made by Guatemalan refugees in Mexico on the grounds that accurate testimony could only be obtained inside Guatemala. Sadly, digging people up for eyewitness testimony posed insurmountable challenges, so the reports from escaped refugees continued to smear the good name of Uncle Sam's Guatemalan security squads.

Tried for lying to Congress, Elliot called the prosecutors "filthy bastards," referred to the proceedings as "Kafkaesque," and denounced the members of the Senate Intelligence Committee as "pious clowns." Flattery was old hat for him. When journalist Terry Allen once told him that much of the world considered him a war criminal, he called her a "rotten bitch."

Departed press secretary Ari Fleischer called Elliot an "outstanding diplomat," also reporting that "the president thinks that [Abrams' criminal conduct] is a matter of the past and was dealt with at the time."

Back in the saddle again, Elliot gave the nod to the April 2002 coup against the hugely popular Chavez government in Venezuela. He undoubtedly has many other exciting plans in store for a South America tilting badly to the Left.

ABRAMS DEFENDS GUATEMALAN ANTI-COMMUNIST CRUSADE

The US role in Guatemala during the 1980s was discussed by Abrams with journalist Allan Nairn in a fond look back aired on the Charlie Rose Show in 1995:

Nairn: *. . . in the face of this systematic policy of slaughter by the Guatemalan military, more than 110,000 civilians killed by that military since 1978, what Amnesty International has called a "government program of political murder," the US has continued to provide covert assistance to the G-2 and they have continued, especially during the time of Mr. Abrams, to provide political aid and comfort. For example . . .*

Abrams: *Uh, Charlie.*

Rose: *One second.*

Nairn: *. . . during the Northwest Highland massacres of the [early] 80s when the Catholic Church said: "Never in our history has it come to such grave extremes. It has reached the point of genocide." President Reagan went down, embraced [General] Rios Montt, the dictator who was staging these massacres, and said he was getting "a bum rap on human rights." In '85 when human rights leader Rosario Godoy was abducted by the army, raped, and mutilated, her baby had his fingernails torn out, the Guatemalan military said: "Oh, they died in a traffic accident." Human rights groups contacted Mr. Abrams, asked him about it, he wrote back—this is his letter of reply—he said: yes, "there's no evidence other than that they died in a traffic accident." Now this is a woman raped and mutilated, a baby with his fingernails torn out. This is long-standing policy.*

Rose: *. . . these are specific points raised by Allan having to do with your public conduct.*

Abrams: *. . . I'm not here to refight the Cold War. I'm glad we won . . .*

Nairn: *Won against who, won against those civilians the Guatemalan army was massacring?*

Abrams: *Wait a minute. Wait a minute. Wait a minute. Wait a minute. We're not here to refight the Cold War. . . . If Mr. Nairn thinks we should have been on the other side in Guatemala, that we should have been in favor of a guerrilla victory, I disagree with him.*

Nairn: *So you're then admitting that you were on the side of the Guatemalan military!*

Abrams: *I am admitting that it was the policy of the United States, under Democrats and Republicans, approved by Congress repeatedly to oppose a Communist guerrilla victory anywhere in Central America including in Guatemala.*

Nairn: *"A Communist guerrilla victory!" Ninety-five percent of these victims are civilians—peasant organizers, human rights leaders, priests—assassinated by the US-backed Guatemalan army.*

Rose: *I'm happy to invite both of you back to review Reagan and Bush [Senior] administration policy. Right now I want to stick to this point . . .*

Nairn: *Let's look at reality here. . . . We're talking about more than a hundred thousand murders, an entire army, many of its top officers employees of the US government. We're talking about crimes and we're also talking about crim-*inals; not just people like Guatemalan Colonels but also the US agents who've been working with them, and the higher level US officials. I mean, I think you have to apply uniform standards. President Bush [Senior] once talked about putting Saddam Hussein on trial for crimes against humanity—Nuremberg style tribunal. I think that's a good idea. But if you're serious, you have to be even-handed. If you look at a case like this, I think we have to* start talking about putting Guatemalan and US officials on trial. I think someone like Mr. Abrams would be a fit subject for such a Nuremberg-style inquiry.

Abrams: *[laughs]*

Nairn: . . . but I agree with Mr. Abrams that Democrats would have to be in the dock with him.

Rose: Well, well I . . . again, I invite you and Elliot Abrams back to discuss what he did, but right now . . .

Abrams: No thanks, Charlie, but . . .

Rose: Elliot, go ahead Elliot, to repeat the question, do you want to be in the dock?

Abrams: It is ludicrous, it is ludicrous to respond to that kind of stupidity. This guy thinks we were on the wrong side in the Cold War. . .

Nairn: Mr. Abrams, you were on the wrong side in supporting the massacre of peasants and organizers and anyone who dared speak. Absolutely. And that's a crime. That's a crime, Mr. Abrams, for which people should be tried. It's against the law.

Abrams: (sarcastically) All right, we'll put all the American officials who won the Cold War in the dock.

Rose: . . . Allan Nairn is a distinguished reporter who won the George Polk Award last year. So, I mean, you know, I don't want him characterized on this broadcast as a crackpot. I mean, you can have a personal argument about what he says about you specifically, but . . .

Abrams: Well, Charlie, Charlie, Charlie, when a guy tells me he thinks the entire US leadership during the Cold War needs to have a Nuremberg trial, he's a crackpot.

Rose: OK, I mean, I, I wouldn't, point well taken.

Nairn: Well, it's Mr. Abrams's right to say whatever he wants, but the facts speak for themselves. And in the case of Guatemala you have this ongoing pattern of murder which has been public record— the Catholic Church in Guatemala has documented it, all the human rights groups have documented it. And on the public level, not even talking about the covert level, year after year the US has continued to provide all different kinds of aid to the Guatemalan military. . .

WE'VE DECIDED ALL THOSE INTERNATIONAL TREATIES WERE JUST TOO DARN CONFUSING. THAT'S WHY WE'RE REPLACING THEM WITH SOME SIMPLE **PRAYERS**! WE CALL IT OUR NEW

Faith Based Foreign Policy

THE NUCLEAR PROLIFERATION PRAYER

God, grant me a really good Anti Ballistic Missile.

Give it the range to hit anything,

And the wisdom to know a warhead from a decoy.

Amen

THE LAND MINE PRAYER

Dear Lord,

May the poor soul who steps on an old land mine not be me.

Amen

THE GLOBAL WARMING PRAYER

Give us this day our big S.U.V's.

Forgive us our emissions

And deliver us from those greenhouse gases

For you are the big mysterious thermostat in the sky.

Amen

SPECIAL PRESIDENTIAL ENVOY FOR LATIN AMERICA IN THE NATIONAL SECURITY COUNCIL

OTTO REICH
AN AMERICAN REICH

A super-patriotic Cuban-American who hates the Cuban revolution, Otto Reich lobbied hard for Elian Gonzalez's inalienable right to live with his kidnappers forever.

He has been completely fed up with the slackness in the US economic embargo against Cuba for a long time, once denouncing a Baltimore Orioles-Cuba baseball game on the grounds that "It trivializes the situation there. It's like playing soccer in Auschwitz."

This is an unfortunate example of Reich's penchant for understatement. Everyone knows Auschwitz was a walk in the park compared to Cuba.

In the 1980s, Reich ran the semi-clandestine Office of Public Diplomacy, which bombarded the American public with assertions that Communism was taking over Central America. One high Reagan Administration official likened the disinformation office to the kind of propaganda operation directed in "enemy territory." Acting as assistant to the distinguished Oliver North, Reich praised the Contras to the skies and was a key player in fundraising on their behalf by swapping arms for hostages with the merry mullahs of Iran.

In the late 1980s he was the US Ambassador to Venezuela, where he showed keen interest in the fate of jailed Cuban-American Orlando Bosch. Bosch had been imprisoned for the 1976 sky-bombing of a Cubana Airlines passenger plane that killed everyone on board, including most of Cuba's national fencing team and an American peace activist. For some reason Venezuelan law frowns on that sort of thing. Anyway, Bosch was released during Reich's ambassadorship and immediately moved to Miami, where he received a full pardon from George Bush Senior. Bosch continues to boast of his airliner downing to this day. Who wouldn't?

When people tell me there are no role-models for kids to look up to anymore, I tell them about Otto Reich. He's a sweetheart and a patriot and a fine human being all rolled into one.

THE TRIUMPH OF THE IDEALISTS

MATTHEWS: *"Let me ask you about military planning. You know, there's a lot of idealists in this administration, people like Paul Wolfowitz of the Defense Department, a very bright guy, a tremendous idealist. He believes that we're out there, as you've probably heard him say this, we're fighting against despotism in the war, we're fighting for liberation of people, like those people in Iraq."*
—Chris Matthews on MSNBC's Hardball (2/24/03)
interviewing Retired General Norman Scwarzkopf

The idealists are back in charge in the executive branch. Pursuing their principled agenda many of these dreamers are picking up a fight that they've been pursuing for years.

Paul Wolfowitz's obsession with the well being of the Iraqi people goes back to the Reagan Administration in which he worked. Perhaps it was there where he discovered the idealism of warfare. Unwavering in his idealism over the years it's instructive to remember that this is one idealist who's always wanted to invade Iraq.

During the Clinton years Wolfowitz was part of an idealistic group of Reaganites who call themselves Project for the New American Century. In a 1997 letter to Clinton, long before 9-11, they were clear on what had to be done with Iraq:

"Given the magnitude of the threat, the current policy, which depends for its success upon the steadfastness of our coalition partners and upon the cooperation of Saddam Hussein, is dangerously inadequate. The only acceptable strategy is one that eliminates the possibility that Iraq will be able to use or threaten to use weapons of mass destruction. In the near term, this means a willingness to undertake military action as diplomacy is clearly failing. In the long term, it means removing Saddam Hussein and his regime from power. That now needs to become the aim of American foreign policy."

Another idealistic compatriot from the Reagan years (and also a principle in Project for the New American Century) has returned too ccupy a couple positions of power within the Bush White House. Elliot Abrams is now a Special Assistant to the President and he brings the same idealism and love of human rights that lead him to help create and then back the Contras in the US secret war on Nicaragua. This idealism was undiminished by the meddlesome US Congress or even the World Court. High-minded Elliot was willing to disobey both in his quest to do anything to help the people of Nicaragua.

For his brave efforts he did have to admit to lying to Congress, a felony, to cover up US complicity in Contra atrocities, but George HW Bush pardoned him along with five other patriotic idealists. Explaining those pardons, Bush said the "common denominator of their motivation—whether their actions were right or wrong—was patriotism."

This band of patriots didn't let international law get in the way of their idealistic pursuits either. The World Court in The Hague attempted to intervene but fortunately the United States excludes all disputes concerning domestic matters from the court's jurisdiction, reserving the right to determine what it regards as domestic. In 1986, it disregarded the court's finding that it had violated Nicaragua's sovereignty. Similarly the Security Council's resolution to halt American aid to the Contras was vetoed by the US. Extremism in the pursuit of idealism is no vice.

Now that they've had their way with Iraq who know what new country will benefit from the blessings of their idealistic campaign. Nothing will slow their demonstrated devotion to political idealism. Nothing.

CHAPTER FOUR

CUT! CUT! DRILL! DRILL! IT'S OFF TO WORK WE GO!

THE TRAIN WRECK LEAVES THE STATION

M. WUERKER

GUT OUR BENEFITS - PLEASE!

Former Treasury Secretary Paul O'Neill hit the nail on the head when he recommended Americans meet all their pension and medical needs by private means. If you can't cover your gall bladder surgery with what you have in savings, do without! Or try self-surgery. But don't expect a government handout for God sakes, Communism is dead and gone.

Anyway, as we all know from civics classes, government should only perform those tasks that Americans cannot perform themselves—like carpet-bombing foreign nations and giving away the store to transnational corporations and international banks. Beyond that, government has no legitimate function. Not to mention that we-the-people are ashamed to accept government help. Rugged individualists, we just want to work ourselves to the bone, pay taxes, and watch our lives go down the drain.

Now, about Medicare, surely King George is correct that HMOs are more efficient than government-funded care. I mean, how much equity is returned to stockholders under Medicare? Absolutely none! Whereas under HMOs investors are making a killing, if you'll pardon the expression. Admitedly, the administrative costs are seven to ten times higher under HMOs, but those are passed on to the public, which needs a little financial discipline to keep it from launching Communist slave initiatives like the New Deal. So let's just get used to rising premiums and shrinking benefits—they're a small price to pay for unrestrained greed.

Privatization of Social Security is equally essential. In the era of Andersen-style "creative accounting" can we really consider any other option? I think not. So just spin that old pension wheel and see WHO ends up with WHAT. If your nest-egg is Enronized and you are dumped in the street at 65, so be it. Just keep your chin up and hustle on down to Burger King. Bagging "freedom fries" for minimum wage is a great way to spend your "Golden Years."

KING GEORGE'S DOWN-HOME, LONE STAR RECIPES

The Menu that Devours Diners

CHICKENHAWK CASSEROLE

Ingredients:
One cabal draft-dodging war-mongers
Large sack of infantile rhetoric
One housebroken press
One ocean of petroleum
One rigged election
String of implausible rationales
Several layers extra-Constitutional powers
Large bag of threats
One mountain of ancient Mesopotamian treasures

Preparation
Skim off voter input with rigged election. Discard.
Wrap cabal of draft-dodging war mongers in extra-Constitutional powers while spoon-feeding infantile rhetoric to housebroken press.
Drop string of implausible rationales into the war mix. Smother laughter with bag of threats. Seize ocean of petroleum firmly while smashing ancient Mesopotamian treasures to rubble. Then burn to a crisp.
Serve with disdain. Middle Easterners automatically entitled to several helpings.

TAX-CUT RHUBARB

Ingredients:
One inherited budget surplus
One bunch unfunded wars
Four dozen bankrupt state governments
Dash of sugary rhetoric

Preparation
Drain national treasury thoroughly. When inherited surplus is completely squandered, immerse country in red ink with tax cuts for the rich in mid-recession.
Use funnel to flood the hundreds of billions of dollars of refunds back to your wealthy benefactors while you line up the series of unfunded wars to make sure the nation remains in hock to them forever.
Sprinkle sugary rhetoric on bankrupt state governments. Serve with Democrat Jello.

SKEWERED ETHICS

Ingredients:
One Manichean world view
One stack lame rationalizations, jumbo size
One Neandarthal staff
One parade Hitler clones
One rhetoric of vengeance
One set ideological blinders
One space-age military

Preparation
Place Manichean world view firmly in public mind using ideological blinders.   Shred nuances thoroughly.
Add in parade of Hitler clones while intoning rhetoric of vengeance. When public is frothing at the mouth, unleash space-age military on civilians ruled by the weakest of the Hitler clones. Ignore body count and immerse the disaster in lame rationalizations provided by Neandarthal staff. Serve with contempt.

PALESTINE STEW

Ingredients:
One demented war criminal
One large accusation of anti-Semitism
One pair of "chosen peoples"
Liberal dose of fundamentalist theology, half-Christian, half-Jewish
One supine Congress, bought and paid for
One stream pundit diarrhea
One captive Palestinian population
Yeasty group of settler-fanatics
One avalanche lethal technology, including nuclear
One ocean American cash

Preparation
Set aside moral concerns. Place "chosen peoples" side by side until ideological fermentation occurs. When the odor of self-righteousness becomes overpowering, take ocean of American cash and buy the Congress. Saturate US tax-payers with pundit diarrhea to prevent public resentment. If resistance emerges crush with accusation of anti-Semitism.
Dump avalanche of lethal technology on demented war criminal and hermetically seal captive Palestinian population in non-contiguous cantons.
Bring stew to a rolling boil. Increase heat and clamp the lid on firmly until explosions occur. Salt wounds with settler fanatics and add fundamentalist theology until you catch a whiff of Armageddon.
Garnish with nukes and serve with hysteria. Ideal for "Last Supper."

CREAMED WAGES

Ingredients:
One demoralized populace
One "flexible" labor market
Several large clumps bloated CEOs
Army of two-faced accountants
One set permanent replacement workers—instant
One Horatio Alger myth
One New Deal
One package consulting fees—extra sweet
One set union organizers
One variety-pack crumpled benefits

Preparation
Soak demoralized populace in "flexible" labor market. Drain hope thoroughly. Slice and dice New Deal to mincemeat while ridiculing all efforts at solidarity. Skin union organizers and gradually stir in bloated CEOs, two-faced accountants, and Horatio Alger myth until layer of scum forms on top of social mixture. Add consulting fees to thicken scum.
Be on guard against dreaded "souffle effect." If wages begin to rise, salt heavily with permanent replacement workers and crumpled benefits. If necessary extract New Deal and union organizers from mixture and mash to a pulp.
Serve with patriotic fanfare.

DEMOCRACY FLAMBEE

Ingredients:
One cabal world-domination specialists
One democratic Constitution
One frightened citizenry
One stream terrifying imagery
One infinitely elastic anti-terror pretext
Ample stock media lickspittles

Preparation
Mix cabal of world-domination specialists with infinitely elastic anti-terror pretext. Stretch pretext to fit every contingency and unleash wars all over the planet.
Marinate frightened citizenry in terrifying imagery while peeling away amendments from the Bill of Rights. When the Constitution is thoroughly gutted announce triumph of liberty. Serve in flames to applause of media lickspittles.

ACCOUNTANT FUDGE

Ingredients:
One large conflict of interest
One commercial banking system
One investment banking system
Several tons phantom revenue
Encyclopedia of accounting gimmicks
Network of salesman-accountants
One package extra large consulting fees
One lapdog media
One set insider pirates
One facade mock confusion

Preparation
Combine commercial and investment banking systems in one large conflict of interest. Grossly inflate cash flow and profits with phantom revenue provided by accounting gimmicks. Baste salesman-accountants in consulting fees while lapdog media butters them up as celebrities of the "New Economy." When their swelling vanity peaks, your books should be thoroughly cooked. Cut into certificate squares and alert insider pirates to cash in just before they become worthless. Serve with mock confusion.

DEMOCRAT JELLO

Ingredients:
1 invertebrate mass from Democratic Leadership Council

Preparation
Use cookie cutter to separate into individual representatives. Grease their palms thoroughly. Store in deep-freeze with bi-annual election check to make sure contents are still bland and tasteless. Serve with canned laughter.

Cooking Up RECORD DEFICITS

Deficits are easy but making 'em out of a big ol' surplus is a challenge... Here's how!

START WITH A BIG FAT BUDGET SURPLUS, SAY... $230 BILLION. THROW IN BIG POT.

COOK IT DOWN, LADDLING OFF HUGE TAX CUTS TO YOUR WEALTHIEST SUPPORTERS

CRANK UP HEAT WITH NEEDLESS WAR, MUSHROOMING MILITARY BUDGET, EXPENSIVE OPEN ENDED OCCUPATION

AND VOILA! YOU'VE GOT A $455 BILLION DEFICIT AND DEFICITS AS FAR AS YOU CAN SEE!

M. WUERKER

KING GEORGE
VS.
THE ENVIRONMENT

He abandoned his campaign pledge to regulate carbon dioxide emissions. He suspended an executive order preventing serial polluters from getting federal contracts. He proposed reversing a ban on road-building in 60 million acres of national forest. He canceled a deadline for auto makers to come up with prototypes for high-mileage cars. He rolled back safeguards for nuclear waste storage. He shifted the clean-up costs for toxic waste Superfund sites from polluters to the public. He blocked a program to check the discharge of raw sewage into America's waters. He sabotaged protections for national parks and monuments. He turned federal energy policy over to Enron.

But back at the ranch he recreated in an "environmentally sensitive showplace" featuring "state-of-the-art energy efficiency" devices and a lawn and orchard irrigated with recycled water.

What's good for King George is bad for America. Praise his holy name!

CHAPTER FIVE

DEJA VOO DOO

ENRONOMICS AND THE NEW CLASS WARFARE

HOW TO GET LAY'D

Note the warm relations that Daddy Bush cultivated when he rewarded Lay with a sleep-over at the White House. Take your cue and treasure this old friend who called you and your wife "George and Laura" long before you ascended to the throne.

Reciprocate for the financial flood Lay has provided you—$275,000 for the GOP in the 2000 election cycle, another $300,000 for the Inaugural festivities, and Enron jets

for your royal staff to gad about in. Appoint him your personal advisor for the post-election "transition."

Make his company your political brain trust, appointing a chief economic advisor that used to be on Enron's payroll, an Enron lobbyist (Marc Racicot) to head the Republican National Committee, a trade representative (Robert Zoellick) that once served on Enron's advisory council, an

Army Secretary (Thomas White) that used to be vice chair of Enron Energy Services. Don't bat an eyelash when White cashes out millions in Enron stock just before the share price collapses. Ditto for Karl Rove and his $100,000 of Enron stock.

Call Lay "Kenny Boy" until the reek of plunder is impossible to ignore. Appoint two Lay favorites to the Federal Energy Regulatory Commission while sweeping away a last-minute Clinton order halting uncontrolled speculation in California's electricity market. Contain your delight when Enron profits soar by $87 million in three months and an "energy crisis" erupts. Have your Vice President repeatedly meet with Lay and agree not to impose legally required price caps that would spare consumers the massive gouging. Recommend that Californians weather the crisis by handing over their tax cuts to your Texas oil and gas buddies.

Craft a national energy plan that reads like an Enron utopia.

ENRON? THEY'RE BIG BACKERS OF ANN RICHARDS ...RIGHT?

O.K. THEY CONTRIBUTED TO OUR ENERGY PLAN... BUT WE DIDN'T INHALE.

DO I KNOW KEN LAY? HOW DO YOU DEFINE "KNOW"?

I DID **NOT** HAVE RELATIONS WITH THAT CORPORATION!!

HOW TO GET SCREWED

Let Enron privatize your electricity and water, as in Britain, where Maggie Thatcher led the way to the Brave New World of privatization. Let water bills soar to 2.5 times the US price while water company stocks quintuple in value. Let a big political donor came out on top as the system crashes—Wessex Water—100% owned by Enron.

Let Enron close a sweetheart deal for a natural gas pipeline with Argentine President Carlos Menem, a close friend of the Bush family. When the Argentine economy collapses due to IMF austerity measures, let them saddle ratepayers with impossible prices linked to the US dollar

Let them add the Buenos Aires water system to their shopping cart, believing their solemn promises to invest right up to the moment they institute mass firings. Let them eliminate budget frills like repairing broken water mains and preventing contamination of the water supply. Have the US taxpayer subsidize the operation through the Inter-American Development Bank.

Let them negotiate a power plant at Dahbol India without competitive bidding or penalty for bad performance—and let it be so astronomically priced it turns out cheaper to pay the fees to keep the plant idle than to let it run and buy the power. Arrange for police to beat the crap out of demonstrators who protest, using Enron helicopters to surveill the crowds. Let the Clinton and Bush Administrations act as Enron collection agents by insisting the company ransom be paid.

Let deregulation reign in California. Let Enron induce rolling blackouts by contracting energy supplies in peak demand periods and let Ken Lay fire the head of the Federal Energy Regulatory Commission for lack of cooperation.

Let electricity prices skyrocket and billions of consumer dollars hemmorhage out of state.

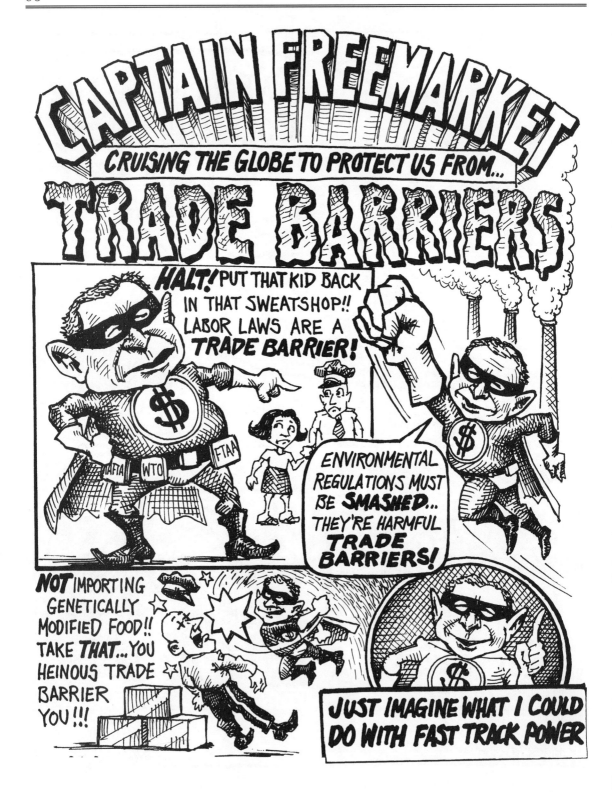

EDUCATION (1): LEAVE NO CHILD UNTRAUMATIZED

King George insists on constant high-stakes testing for those lacking the foresight to be born rich.

Make-or-break standardized tests foster fear, which we know is the best teacher. Kids who are anxious, stressed-out, and terrified of failing are destined for success in rat-race living. Plus, year-round regurgitation of pre-packaged "right" answers kills off curiosity, which helps "motivate achievement," according to the Education Excellence Partnership. And achievement is measured by—you guessed it!—doing well on tests.

See, students in our "failing schools" (i.e. holding pens for hordes of blacks and Latinos) just don't "know enough," owing to sixties permissiveness and its weakening effect on curriculum, assessment standards, and the moral fiber of the nation. The solution is no-nonsense,

tough standards, which will make the students "motivated" (i.e. scared shitless) to learn. The "higher" standards will lift poor children out of the "culture of poverty" to university study, where they will work like galley slaves, accumulate massive debt, graduate to a crappy job market, work like galley slaves again, and pay off their college loans before dying flat broke like their parents and their parents before them.

Well, that's what happens if everything goes well. If things don't go well, armies of drop-outs get swallowed up by poverty, disease, drug-addiction, and despair, spending a large portion of their lives in prison. There they have lots of time to earn their high school diploma, which is a very valuable document, especially attached to a prison record.

If they're on death row, at least they die knowing the society that killed them cared enough to half-educate them.

EDUCATION (2): WHEN THEY'RE DOWN, STOMP ON 'EM

As a society, it's important we perfect this sequence. First, cultivate poverty, which guarantees the educational disaster we all know and love. Then, when pitiful test scores confirm the obvious, punish the impoverished schools by cutting anemic funding levels further while threatening them with still worse if they don't improve their scores. Results will continue to deteriorate, which will justify further spending cuts. And don't forget to return tax money for use as vouchers to parents whose kids attend "failing schools," so the

better off among them can attend private or religious schools. This sinks the worst-off schools even deeper in bankruptcy and reinforces the message to the students stuck there that they are less than worthless. Lots of young people are irreparably damaged, educators are plunged into despair, and a new generation of apprentice criminals hits the streets, which justifies more investment in the run-away prison construction boom. It's a win-win situation all the way around.

THE LEVEL PLAYING FIELD

M. WUERKER

KING GEORGE'S ECONOMIC HALL OF FAME

1) Hall of Famer:
Fed Chairman,
Alan Greenspan

Bushevik achievement: Hailed as a God for steering the 1990s fairy tale economy, whose narrowly distributed gains he credited to "greater worker insecurity."

Classic witticism: "The stock market, as best as I can judge, is high. It's not that there is a bubble in there."
—Federal ReserveMeeting, May 1996

2) Hall of Famer:
Dick Cheney

Bushevik achievement: CEO of Halliburton when it listed anticipated cost overruns on Pentagon and other contracts as current profits, overstating its revenues by hundreds of millions of dollars in order to inflate the company's share price. The company auditor was Aurthur Andersen.

Classic witticism: "I get good advice, if you will, from their [Arthur Andersen] people based upon how we're doing business and how we're operating, over and above the normal, by-the-book auditing arrangement."
—Cheney on Arthur Andersen video, 1996

3) Hall of Famer:
WorldCom CEO,
Bernie Ebbers

Bushevik achievement: Under his stewardship the company overstated its earnings by $7 billion, the largest accounting fraud in history and six times the size of Enron's. On news of its "restatement," WorldCom stock plunged 93% to close at six cents a share. Telecom investors lost $180 billion.

A few days before the WorldCom disaster became public, the company donated $100,000 to the Republicans at a gala attended by King George. The responsibility for investigating the fraud falls to John Ashcroft, who received $10,000 from WorldCom when he ran for Senator.

Classic witticism: "WorldCom has a solid base of bill-paying customers, strong fundamentals, a solid balance sheet, manageable leverage, and nearly $10 billion in available liquidity. Bankruptcy or a credit default is not a concern."
—Ebbers, conference call to investors, February 2002

4) Hall of Famer:
Enron CEO, Ken Lay

Bushevik achievement: A close person friend of King George, he led an executive charge to cash out over $1 billion in company stock, divesting his 4000 employees of their life savings and tossing them into the street for the 2001 year-end holidays. Lay escaped with his wealth intact, including two multi-million dollar vacation homes in Aspen.

Classic witticism: To Enron employees as he looted their pensions: "I want to assure you that I have never felt better about the prospects for the company. Our performance has never been stronger; our business model has never been more robust; our growth has never been more certain." Classic employee rejoinder: "I'd like to know if you're on crack."

5) Hall of Famer:
Tyco CEO, Dennis Kozlowski

Bushevik achievement: With New York digging out from a post 9-11 budget deficit, he stole $1 million in public money (sales tax evasion) while looting $600 million more from the company trough. Tyco shareholders lost $92 billion in market value as the company's stock price plunged 75%.

Classic witticisms: (1) "There are no restatements coming from Tyco, no irregularities, no investigations nor reasons for any investigations." *Bloomberg News*, October 14, 1999

M. WUERKER

(2) "You will be confronted with questions every day that test your morals. Think carefully, and for your sake, do the right thing, not the easy thing."
— from Kozlowski's commencement address at New Hampshire's St. Anselm's College, May 2002, three weeks before he resigned in disgrace

6) Hall of Famer:

Former SEC Chairman Harvey Pitt

Bushevik achievement: Lobbied the SEC to make it easier for Arthur Andersen and other big accounting firms to cook the books for corporate behemoths intent on robbing billions from their employees' pensions and 401(k) plans. When Congress asked for his suggestions on corporate responsibility legislation, Pitt asked for a raise and a cabinet-level position alongside Colin Powell and John Ashcroft.

Classic witticisms:
(1)"[A] kinder, gentler agency."
—Pitt, soon after taking office, on his vision for the SEC
(2)"A firm that does only audits may be incompetent."
—- Pitt, on accounting firms that don't cook the books to earn fat consulting fees.

GUARDING THE HEN HOUSE

H. PITT

CHENEY

BUSH MOVES TO CLEAN UP WALL ST....

7) Hall of Famer:
King of the Planet, George W. Bush, MBA

Bushevik achievements: After receiving large campaign contributions from Enron and MCI/WorldCom, he indicated his gratitude to Harvey Pitt, who had made it easier for such firms to engage in "creative accounting" by appointing him head of the SEC. Then, with the accounting scandal in full swing, he brought down the house at a White House press conference by stating that accounting wasn't all black and white.

Classic witticisms:

(1) "If they [the public] buy stock, they're buying value—as opposed to buying . . . into a bubble."

(2) "I believe people have taken a step back and asked, 'What's important in life?' You know, the bottom line and this corporate America stuff—is that important? Or is serving your neighbor, loving your neighbor like you'd like to be loved yourself?"

8) Hall of Famer:
Jack Grubman, Prince of Telecom

Bushevik achievement: Kept his "buy" rating on Global Crossing as it dove from $61 a share to $1.07, finally changing it to "neutral." The resulting bankruptcy was the fourth largest in US history, wiping out $57 billion in shareholder value and 9,000 jobs.

Classic witticisms: (1) "WorldCom is the one I would buy because it has the least execution risk to get back going, the best set of assets, the best revenue mix, and the best balance sheet . . ."
—Fortune, December 18, 2000
(2) "What used to be a conflict is now a synergy. Someone like me who is banking-intensive would have been looked at disdainfully by the buy side

fifteen years ago. Now they know I'm in the flow of what's going on."
—May 15, 2000

9) Hall of Famer:
Enron President and CEO Jeffrey Skilling

Bushevik achievement: At the top of a company that gave nearly $1.3 million to the GOP in 2000, he escaped with $100 million in stock options, leaving workers to face financial ruin. He still maintains he "made the right decisions."

Classic witticisms:
(1) "We have a better business model. It's a fundamentally better business model."
—November 6, 2000
(2) "I am resigning for personal reasons. I want to thank Ken Lay for his understanding of this purely personal decision."
—August 14, 2001
(3) On the witness stand before Congress, he repeated seven times:
"I am not an accountant."

— M. WUERKER —

10) Hall of Famer:
Gerald Levin
AOL Time Warner CEO

Bushevik achievement: Averaged $45 million annual compensation when putting together merger of AOL and Time-Warner. After the deal went through, AOL stock plummeted from $50 to $9.

Classic witticism: (Resigning): "I want to put the poetry back in my life."

←————————————→

11) Hall of Famer:
John Rigas,
Founder Adelphi Communications

Bushevik achievement: Ripped off $3.1 billion from his shareholders by inflating earnings and hiding debt. Federal prosecutors charged that Rigas and his nepotism ring "looted Adelphia on a massive scale using the company as the Rigas family's personal piggy bank." They concluded that it represented "one of the most elaborate and extensive corporate frauds in US history." Rigas' direction of the company produced a 99% decline in Adelphia's stock price, wiping out some $6 billion in shareholder equity.

Classic witticism: "Adelphia has positioned itself very well for the future. . . . We're here for the long pull because we think there is a lot of value and it's a great business."
—February 15, 2001

←————————————→

12) Hall of Famer:
Joseph Nacchio,
CEO and Chairman,
Qwest Communications

Bushevik achievement: Laid off over 7,000 employees while engineering Qwest's stock price plunge of 98% between March 2000 and August 2002. He then blamed "Enronitis" and "corporate McCarthyism" for the disaster, reasoning that "if things weren't in the press, they wouldn't have asked."

Classic witticism:
"We're doing what we get paid to do."

←————————————→

13) Hall of Famer:
Bush Chief Economic
Adviser Lawrence Lindsey

Bushevik achievement: First blamed massive market decline on "anti-business" philosophy of Al Gore during 2000 campaign, then a "hangover" from the 1990s stock market bubble once Bush became president.

Classic witticism: On Enron disaster: "A tribute to American capitalism."

14) Hall of Famer:
Clinton Treasury Secretary, Robert Rubin

Bushevik achievement: Helped repeal the Glass-Steagall Act so that Travelers Insurance could buy Citicorp. After leaving government he got a job with the company. From there he put in a call to a top credit rating agency and the Bush Department of Treasury in an effort to delay the down-grading of Enron's credit rating, allowing it to defraud the public for a few more frantic weeks.

Classic witticism: On the Enron rescue call: "I would do it again."

Ken Lay
c/o George W. Bush
The White House
Washington D.C.

Dear Mr. Lay,

Everyone says you represent success in the Bush years, so I'm hoping you can offer me career advice.

The career counselor at school recommends "doing what you love." That's got me wondering what you love most: buying politicians, defrauding workers, swindling customers, robbing shareholders, or plundering impoverished Third World countries?

I think you're a PR genius. I really admire your line about Jesus being a libertarian because he wanted people to have choices. Do you think it's O.K. to say Buddha was a neoconservative because he wanted everyone to be "liberated"?

One thing I need help with is lying. I envy you for having told your employees, "The company is fundamentally sound" just when Enron stock was set to collapse. And it was pure genius to hold that company-wide electronic Town Hall meeting and instruct the employees to, "Talk up the stock and talk positively about Enron to your family and friends" right when you were looting their pensions. I'm afraid pangs of conscience would cause me to throw up in a situation like that. Any advice on how to overcome this?

By the way, bravo to you for that phony energy crisis you cooked up in California. Monopolize supplies, then deregulate the market. Nice! You ripped off billions from those tree-huggers and all-electric idiots in Silicon Valley. You're the best.

Well, gotta run. Tell George that Andersen Accounting has his approval rating at 138%. He's a shoo-in for several more terms.

Best,

Randy North

DEJA VOO DOO

CHAPTER SIX

BUSHWHACKING THE PLANET

OPERATION ENDURING ENEMIES

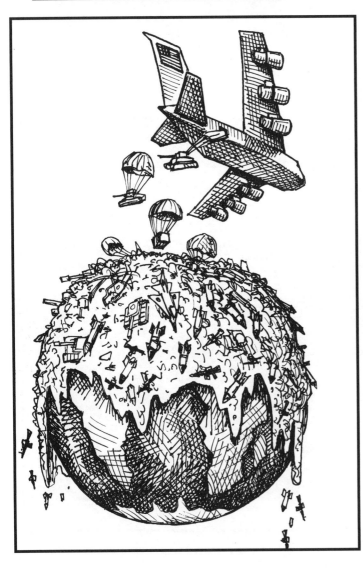

"We must make clear to the Germans that the wrong for which their fallen leaders are on trial is not that they lost the war, but that they started it. And we must not allow ourselves to be drawn into a trial of the causes of the war, for our position is that no grievances or policies will justify resort to aggressive war. It is utterly renounced and condemned as an instrument of policy."

—US Supreme Court Justice Robert L. Jackson, Chief US Prosecutor at the Nuremberg Tribunal August 12, 1945

April 17, 2003
The Honorable Donald Rumsfeld
1000 Defense Pentagon
Washington, D.C. 20301-1000

Dear Mr. Secretary,

Congratulations on your speedy triumph over the Iraqi evildoers. Never have I been so proud to be an American. To watch the vegetable markets explode and hear the havoc-ridden shrieks of Iraqi mothers was a great satisfaction to me, and I'm sure, to all patriotic Americans. Thank you so much.

I know you have your hands full presiding over the smashing, burning, and looting of 8,000 years worth of cultural treasures in the Baghdad Museum, and I quite agree that the whole story is just a lot of media hype, but I wonder if you might tell me if there is any chance of my moving to the scene of the mayhem at the earliest possible moment? All this talk of a bill of rights, self-rule, freedom of speech and religion, equality before the law, checks and balances, protection for minorities, and government chosen by and responsive to the people is making me quite antsy to experience this democracy business first-hand. My grandfather has told me the incredible story of how this form of government actually existed in the USA in the Pre-Terror Era, that is, long ago. This is certainly difficult to believe. I'm quite sure Attorney General Ashcroft would not approve of it. I guess I should turn Grandpa in, right?

Whatever the case may be as far as the past, I'm real eager to pay a visit to Baghdad USA. right away. Do I have to enlist or can I just buy a ticket at Expedia.com and be on my way?

Of course, my parents are urging me to stay right here at home, swearing that democracy will be revived soon in the United States. But they came of age in the 1960s and you know how incredibly over-optimistic that generation was. A lot of them still think pot will be legal someday. I'll get you a list of names if you want.

Anyway, I break out in goosebumps every time I think of your achievement: An entirely new government chosen by the US military, based on who has "cooperated" with our conquest. Brilliant! I know we also need armies of stool pigeons to help Tom Ridge here at home, but I really think I'm better suited to teaching Iraqis how to be good Americans. Now that their cultural heritage has been obliterated it should be all downhill.

Do you have any need for assistant viceroys? If so, I volunteer.

Keep up the good work!

Your biggest fan,
Andy Asskisser

FEEDING THE HUNGRY

Widely hailed as a Free Market success story, Argentina's economy crashed into disaster just before Christmas 2001. Hungry mobs began looting the supermarkets and in the widening chaos blood was shed. Soon crowds throughout the country were pouring into the streets banging ladles on pots and pans to protest that cupboards were bare. Even after the police opened fire they refused to disperse. The government collapsed.

King George instantly perceived a solution to the problem. He insisted the new Argentine government carry out a program of "greater austerity." The bankers' wallets must be filled, said George, but hungry bellies not.

The Argentines proved a stubborn lot. They refused to eat their pots.

PROGRESS REPORT ON HOMELAND SECURITY

Although we are making substantial headway on destroying the freedom that Al Qaeda hates us for, there's still a long way to go and resentment levels remain high.

This is primarily because Arab and Muslim peoples are neurotically sensitive about being blockaded, bombed, strafed, occupied, and terrorized by Washington and its proxies. US research psychologists are puzzled by this reaction and have to date uncovered no clue as to why Americans aren't universally adored. They are adjusting appropriately by getting more selective in their pursuit of the facts and will soon only admit data that confirms their hypothesis—that Americans are uniquely lovable. The terrorist threat should disappear entirely after that.

In the meantime, the Bush Administration continues to take prudent security measures like imposing a bloody occupation on Iraq, plotting a coup against Iran, and blocking all investigation of Israeli war crimes. Though this has failed to stem the rising tide of anti-American hatred to date, their resolve is firm and they expect it will work out well any day now.

WHY THEY SHOULDN'T HATE US

Countering Irrational Arab and Muslim Grievances Against Liberation by the US

False Grievance #1: Occupied Palestine

Israel's occupation of Palestine is simply self-defense against terrorist maniacs. Consider it from a logical point of view. If I took over your house to liberate me and my family from homelessness and you showed your poor manners by failing to take it in stride, and then after years of shooting up the place I finally decided out of the goodness of my heart to let you live in shackles in the basement, you would have no reason not to cheerfully accept your fate, would you? Of course, you wouldn't. And if you then took it upon yourself to attack me instead, I'd be justified in torturing and killing you in order to preserve the peace and security of the neighborhood, wouldn't I? Of course I would. See how simple it all is when you stop and apply a little reason to the situation?

So what is this tiresome nonsense about Palestinian RIGHTS? How can terrorist maniacs have rights?

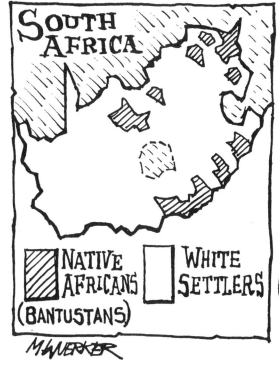

False Grievance #2: US support for reactionary dictators

It's difficult to understand how this could bother anybody. First of all, look at the Persian Gulf region. Other than oil, there's not much economically to exploit. And once that resource runs out, the people are screwed if they haven't developed a modern economy. So just how exactly can we get a democratic majority to support siphoning off the

region's one resource to underwrite an extravagant consumer lifestyle in the West, a policy that will leave the Arab states bankrupt and undeveloped in the not too distant future? The answer is, we can't. So that means we have no choice but to heap arms and aid on repressive dictators who fill up the graveyards with those who have the poor sense to resist US control of the region while the Arab masses endure wretched poverty awaiting the future catastrophe we are steering them toward.

How can anyone get angry about that?

False Grievance #3: Iran

Here's a case where an elected government actually DID try to take control of its own oil in the interests of the people. The CIA engineered a coup (1953) and the people found themselves swimming in blood instead of oil. The pro-Western Shah took over and achieved quite an impressive record of supermilitarization, forced modernization, and systematic torture. Amnesty International rated his human rights record the worst in the world and he almost sank into the sea from the massive load of armaments sent on by Washington.

Then after the Shah was overthrown in 1979, the US supported Saddam Hussein in his eight-year war against Iran, which included the use of chemical weapons. In 1988, the USS Vincennes shot down an Iranian civilian plane and killed 290. George Bush Sr. said: "I'll never apologize for the United States of America. I don't care what the facts are."

All of this was for the best of motives, but "militant Islam" has brainwashed Muslims into hating us for no reason at all. There's no telling when they'll get over it.

False Grievance #4 : Permanent US Military Presence

It's hard to see how this item even got on the list. Would we mind if the United States was dotted with the military bases of a foreign power come to liberate us? Of course, we wouldn't. We would greet our occupiers as liberators and strew their path with flowers. We would be polite and respectful as armed 18-year-olds barged into

our living room and ordered us about in a strange tongue. We would make do without water or electricity or decent food and happily accept the machine-gunning of loved ones as they drove across town.

We would do all this because history shows that military invasions are all about improving the lives of the invaded and we would appreciate being among the beneficiaries.

GIVING AFRICA THE BUSINESS

These billions of dollars in humanitarian aid to Africa George has promised worry me. I think he's backsliding on his commitment to free enterprise, which just doesn't allow for handouts to anyone, AIDS orphans included. It's a little disappointing.

He started off with such promise, appointing the inimitable Andrew Natsios as chief of the US Agency for International Development. Natsios admitted that AIDS was "decimating entire societies," then added with delightful candor that as far as remedies were concerned USAID just "cannot get it done."

Warming to his "it's all hopeless" theme, Natsios declared antiretroviral drugs wasted on Africans, since they "don't know what Western time is" and therefore can't be trusted to take regular medication. Some naiveniks then contended that sun-up and sun-down could serve as reminders of twice daily medication times, but Natsios shrewdly perceived that Africans were just too darn unsophisticated to take medicine and that was that.

Natsios went on to reduce the entire AIDS crisis to a matter of fundamentalist sexual morality, calling for "abstinence, faithfulness and the use of condoms." Of course, this did nothing for the legions already dying of AIDS or the millions of children orphaned by the disease, but it did promote self-denial, an ethic ideally suited to a war-ravaged continent teeming with hungry and diseased people.

Unfortunately, Natsios had to move on and help liberate Iraq, which left George in a bad way on the Africa challenge. The basic problem is that treating 30 million people with AIDS and/or HIV is expensive. Drugs that keep HIV/AIDS patients alive in the US were costing $10,000 a year by the late 1990s. Of course, Indian pharmaceuticals are able to produce generic equivalents for less than $250, but I think everyone understands the injustice involved here. To whit: if free competition is permitted to reign, US pharmaceuticals could be ripped off up to $9750 per patient per year. I don't think Africans have any right to go around robbing good American companies like that.

You may be thinking—isn't free competition what George always insists he is FOR? You're right, he DOES say that, but he only means it when his wealthy benefactors are positioned to win the competition. When they aren't, he's in favor of "property rights," that is, protectionism.

That's why the US tried to block implementation of the World Trade Organization's 2001 Doha Agreement calling for a loosening of patent rules to facilitate generic exports. Negotiators openly admitted to journalists that US resistance to generics was due to pressure from the pharmaceutical lobby, which was only trying to do the right thing—protect their patents no matter how many people died.

George is also promoting economic development in Africa, generous man that he is. Fortunately, he has the wisdom not to funnel aid through international relief agencies or the UN, which are filled with foreigners entirely ignorant of the American way of life and its superiority to all other cultures, traditions, and habits of living. He sends "development assistance" through his Millennium Challenge Account instead, which determines eligibility according to data provided by Africa-friendly institutions like the World Bank, International Monetary Fund, Freedom House, and *Institutional Investor Magazine*. Thanks to their economic policies, average life expectancies on the continent have fallen by 15 years over the past two decades while $15 billion a year in African debt service flows into Western capitals. And all this without a single word of input from African institutions, which are deemed irrelevant to assessing African conditions. After all, what do they know about handling American money?

By the way, Americans have quite a stake in US policy in Africa. The same drug firms that are blocking access to cheap generics for Africans have been fighting for years to keep Medicare from including a prescription drug benefit. This clearly shows the fair-mindedness of the pharmaceuticals, who are striving diligently to make live-saving drugs equally unaffordable to all.

What could be fairer than that?

FAMILY PLANNING

FAITH BASED FAMILY PLANNING

King George's International Fan Club Sends Its Love...

"What I am condemning is that one power, with a president who has no foresight, who cannot think properly, is now wanting to plunge the world into a holocaust."

—Nelson Mandela, January 30, 2003

"Totally an asshole."

—Japanese Foreign Minister Makiko Tanaka describing Bush, June 2001

"What a moron."

—Canadian Communications Director, Francie Ducros, reaction to Bush, 2002

"Bush wants to distract attention from his domestic problems. That's a popular method. Even Hitler did that."

—German Justice Minister, Herta Daeubler-Gmelin

"Damn Americans. I hate those bastards."

—Canadian MP Carolyn Parrish, reaction to the Bush Administration

"I think this [Bush Administration] is the worst government the US has ever had in its more than 200 years of history. It has engaged in extraordinarily irresponsible policies not only in foreign and economic but also in social and environmental policy. This is not normal government policy. Now is the time for people to engage in civil disobedience."

—George A. Akerlof, one of three Nobel Prize winners in economics for 2001

The following is a timely debate on the wisdom of relying on so-called "low-yield" nuclear weapons to "take out" WMD caches held by really bad people, which excludes us of course. In keeping with the tradition of bipartisan consensus in our flawless democracy, non-nuclear options have been ruled out in advance, so don't bother thinking about them.

MINI-NUKES "YES"

First-Strike With "Teeny" Nukes Defines Real Peace
by Harry Scenario

In his umpteenth stroke of pure genius King George has determined that mini-nukes are the answer to the WMD proliferation problem, which has long posed the vexing "Goldilocks Dilemma" for national security strategists. To whit: conventional weapons are too weak to serve as bunker-busters and existing nukes are too strong. Only mini-nukes are just right. They destroy WMD sites but limit collateral damage, affording us the opportunity to extend the preventive war doctrine to cover first-strike nuclear attacks. For you Vietnam era folks, stand by to hear the Pentagon announce: "We had to nuke the country to save it."

Just consider how well this would have worked out in Iraq. Instead of invading and getting bogged down in sandstorms, we could have just let loose with nukes on the 40-odd sites we suspected contained weapons of mass destruction. Of course, this approach presupposes infallible intelligence data, but the Bush Administration clearly has that. So everything would have worked out swell, even better than the invasion did, which has certainly been pleasant enough.

Still, many doubting Thomases fear that an aggressive mini-nukes policy will encourage the proliferation it is designed to prevent. Their reasoning is that new nuclear weapons, resumed testing to develop them, new missions, lowered barriers to first-use, and the Bush Administration's "operational" national missile defense site going up in Fort Greeley, Alaska, will encourage rogue states to develop and use weapons of mass destruction before they are attacked.

But this doesn't really matter because we can nuke their nukes in a first strike and then threaten to annihilate them with a second strike if they don't surrender. If they somehow manage to get one or two missiles in the air, our space shield will slap them down, after which we'll all live happily ever after. It's never worked in practice, but it's sure to pan out in the field. Besides, it's lucrative as hell for major investors in the militarized high-tech sector, and who else really counts?

The Bush Administration is courageously advancing a plan to rid the planet of WMD by stockpiling limitless quantities of WMD. Let's gut the remains of the New Deal and Great Society to help them pay for it. After all, that's what patriotism is all about.

MINI NUKES "NO"
"Low-Yield" Nukes = Shrunken Balls
by Dick Long

William Laurence, witnessing the atomic bombing of Nagasaki, described the Manhattan Project's climax in words that would have pleased Larry Flynt had he been in business at the time: "Then, just when it appeared as though the thing had settled down into a state of permanence, there came shooting out of the top a giant mushroom that increased the size of the pillar to a total of 45,000 feet. The mushroom top was even more alive than the pillar, seething and boiling in a white fury of creamy foam, sizzling upward and then descending earthward, a thousand geysers rolled into one."

Pragmatic planners of American Empire were quick to grasp the erotic nature of the new technology. Bernard Brodie wrote a paper comparing nuclear war with sex, equating the Strategic Air Command's plans for an all-out nuclear attack on the USSR with "going all the way." He properly disdained the reluctance to target cities —on the grounds that it was a form of withdrawal before ejaculation. Meanwhile, colleague and RAND theorist Herman Kahn developed a 44-rung nuclear "escalation ladder," ridiculing SAC's all-or-nothing targeting scheme as a "war orgasm." Though his own G-spot was galaxy destroying machines, he settled for merely terrestrial war in outlining plans for World Wars III, IV, V, VI, VII, and VIII, which included an anticipated evacuation of the country "two or three times every decade."

Unfortunately, America's libidinous nuclear tradition is now threatened by the Bush Administration's pitiful utilitarianism, which calls for "low yield" nukes targeted on military sites like chemical weapons caches. For all its talk of robust bunker busters and "earth penetrators," the Bush Administration is waving a nuclear dildo, and rather limply, in restricting our national sexual outlet to tactical nukes and limited strikes, humiliating options clearly unsuited to a superpower in the age of Viagra. However the Administration may try to hide the truth behind macho rhetoric, Washington's nuclear thrust is clearly decelerating, representing by now no more than nuclear petting in a world fully capable of space war.

The dismal logic of Bush's national security elites would have us believe that region-busters are obsolete because they lack "credibility!" According to this flaccid outlook, rogue states and nuclear outlaws will suspect a bluff if we threaten to annihilate whole regions in our effort to destroy WMD sites, so we must content ourselves with low-yield nukes that can do no more than take out a city or two. Rather than disabuse our enemies of the insulting notion that we are reluctant to destroy all life on earth, today's chicken-hawks retreat to the shameful rhetoric of "small is beautiful."

This child-like eagerness to minimize damage in pursuit of "credibility" overlooks the fact that lust is not divisible and cannot find a satisfactory form of "limited" expression—just ask any junior high school student. The Bush Doctrine, while admirable in its willingness to attack without provocation any nation it does not like, is nevertheless retrogressive on American nuclear sexuality, which simply must return to maximum megatonnage —the only policy affording full gratification.

120

President George W. Bush
1600 Pennsylvania Avenue
The White House
Washington D.C.

Dear Mr. President,

Congratulations on your progress in ridding the world of evildoers. It was thrilling to witness the attack on Saddam's victims, whom he tortured for decades after being helped into power by the C.I.A., supplied with biological weapons materials by an American company, and fully supported by Washington during and after his gassing of Iran and the Kurds. Thank you.

I must confess to disappointment, however, at our abandonment of free market principle. I refer, of course, to Secretary Rumsfeld's shocking denunciation of Syrian entrepreneurs selling night vision goggles to the evil-beyond-description Iraqis. We all know how deadly such items can be to American soldiers forced to make do with an arsenal of satellite-guided missiles, but still, it DOES seem to contradict the fundamental Republican commitment to free-trade-as-liberty.

Even more disturbing is this matter of giving things away for free. I am simply appalled that Hugh Hefner opened his websites without charge so our trained killers could get their rocks off as they heroically liberated the Iraqi people from their desire to live free of foreign occupation. If this keeps up some do-gooder will soon send an avalanche of free dildoes to our women in the trenches. The right approach was demonstrated by our forcing Iraqis to pay for water. Capitalizing on desperate need—that's the American way.

In this regard, you might alert Vice President Cheney that there's a killing to be made in the fissionable materials market via Iran and Pakistan, where a considerable uptick in demand has been noted since you launched your invasion —oops, I mean liberation—of Iraq.

Looking forward to your next dozen wars,

Todd Davis

Satisfied Taxpayer

FINALIZING HIS INVASION PLANS, GEORGE W. BUSH (THE MAN WHO SAID HIS FAVORITE PHILOSOPHER WAS JESUS) PAUSES TO CONSIDER A QUESTION....

DAISY CUTTERS?

CRUISE MISSILES?

CLUSTER BOMBS?

What Would Jesus Drop?

M. WUERKER

THE DEVIL'S TOOLSHED

AXES OF EVIL

THE WHEELBARROW OF *WICKEDNESS*

MALLETS OF MALFEASANCE

BROOMS OF BEELZEBUB

CHAPTER SEVEN

CARTE BLANCHE

MAKING THE MOST OF EVILDOERS

1940 America gets entangled in the Middle East because of its appetite for oil

2001 America is attacked by terrorists mad about its Middle East entanglements

America responds to being attacked...

THIS'LL SHOW EM!...

with record car sales!

ODE TO 9-11

The World Trade Center's collapsed, thousands are dead, the Pentagon's hit, too, four hijacked American planes have plunged to fiery doom with hundreds aboard.

Be Alert! Don't Panic! Go Shopping!

Anthrax keeps killing and no one is willing to handle the letters of death. The Emmy's are canceled, the Congress adjourns, the Supreme Court's closed down, the State Department and Department of Agriculture, too.

Be Alert! Don't Panic! Go Shopping!

The war on terror is a raging success, announces President Buffalo Bill in a sea of American flags. The "evildoers" are routed and rubble is bouncing around starving Afghanistan. Patriots are united in joy.

Be Alert! Don't Panic! Go Shopping!

Relief workers beg for a bombing halt, warning of millions slated to die. The Pentagon's sensitive avengers drop food packets along with their bombs. Bon Appetit!

Be Alert! Don't Panic! Go Shopping!

The economy tanks, interest rates fall flat, billions flow to downsizing corporations, more tax cuts for the rich are proposed. Social security is raided, we can't leave the Fortune 500 unaided, in this hour of national need.

Be Alert! Don't Panic! Go Shopping!

We're number one, God Bless America, together we can save a life, chorus the talking heads on TV. Flanked by grim-faced officials John Ashcroft warns of the umpteenth disaster: Extra double-plus super-duper alert! Terrorist attack imminent!

Be Alert! Don't Panic! Go Shopping!

126

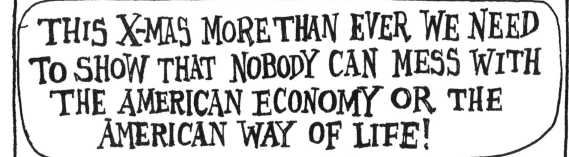

DIAGNOSING EVIL
WHY WE HAD TO TAKE OUT SADDAM

It wasn't about oil. Remember that. Forty-one members of the Bush Administration have ties to the oil industry but the war in Iraq was not about oil. Condoleezza Rice is a former Chevron executive and had an oil tanker named after her but there was no oil motive behind the US takeover in the Persian Gulf, where two-thirds of the world's proven oil reserves coincidentally lie. Sure, Dick Cheney was the advance man for Halliburton but it never colored his judgment about the Middle East. And the flurry of meetings with oil executives at the White House in the weeks preceding the US invasion were simply discussions with private citizens interested in promoting good government. Oil never even came up.

The important point is that SADDAM was an evil man. Evil. Evil. Evil. Horrible. Sickening. Depraved. He controlled fully one-third of the territory of Iraq and wanted more. He was under constant surveillance and surrounded by powerful enemies that for some reason didn't feel threatened by him, but we had to take him out. Had to. Twelve years of bombing and economic blockade had killed over a million Iraqis and strengthened SADDAM's grip on power, but that's just an accident. We always had the best interests of the Iraqi people at heart.

There's no question SADDAM had WMD. We had proof he bought chemical and biological weapons materials. In fact, a 1994 Report of the Senate Banking Committee traced the transactions to their source. It showed that this evil man bought his devilish weapons from innocent American corporations with export licenses to sell him everything he needed. We had the receipts for his anthrax and VX gas and other deadly materials and it was so frightening because he could no longer be trusted to strike the right targets!

But SADDAM had proven himself evil many years before. He got the CIA to support his rise to power, arranged for a financial flood from Washington to prop himself up for decades, and contracted to receive an avalanche of US arms. Have you ever heard of anything more fiendish, wicked, and diabolical?

SADDAM was clearly a threat to world peace, no matter how untroubled his neighbors were. Daddy Bush said he was worse than Hitler and that's pretty bad. If there's any justice that little story of Auschwitz will just fade into insignificance now.

Anyway, Hussein simply could not be trusted. We knew this because we had ominous looking cartoons sketched by the State Department showing Iraq as a haven for terrorists. We also had grainy photographs showing an Al Qaeda training camp in Iraq. Evil! Danger! Horror!

The training camp was right smack in the middle of Kurdish Iraq in the area of the US no fly zone. It was horrible. Hussein simply had to be taken out.

MORE COLLECTED WISDOM OF GEORGE W. BUSH

He-Should-Talk Department

[A] "society that has romanticized violence."
—GW, assigning blame for the Columbine massacre, April 1999

The Great Sandbox Speech:
GW Rebukes Moral Relativism

"Some people think it's inappropriate to draw a moral line in the sand. Not me."
—GW, 2000

Actually You Gave Them $43 Million

"I gave them [the Taliban] a fair chance."
—GW Bush

Osama, the Anthrax Killer, Saddam, Still At Large

"Whether we bring our enemies to justice or bring justice to our enemies, justice will be done."
—GW, 9-20-01

M. WUERKER

GW Does Diplomacy (1)

"Kim Jong Il is a pygmy."
—GW, May 2002

GW Does Diplomacy (2)

"I loathe Kim Jong Il."
—GW to Bob Woodward, August, 2002 at his ranch in Crawford Texas

Big Lie Department

"I hope this [Iraq situation] will not require military action."
—GW, October 7, 2002

Restoring Honesty and Integrity

"I'm the commander, see... I do not need to explain why I say things. That's the interesting thing about being President... (I) don't feel like I owe anybody an explanation."
—GW interview by Bod Woodward

Tender-Loving Destruction

"We must apply our conservative and free-market ideas to the job of helping real human beings. . . . There must be kindness in our justice. There must be mercy in our judgment. There must be a love behind our zeal."

—GW, on religio-politics

How Many Are Our Ex-Employees?

"Thousands of dangerous killers, schooled in the methods of murder . . . are now spread throughout the world like ticking time bombs . . ."
—GW, State of the Union Address, 2003

Thank God We Don't Think Like That

"These [terrorist] enemies view the entire world as a battlefield."
—GW, State of the Union Address, 2003

Say What?

"America has no empire to extend . . ."
—GW, 6-01-02 West Point.

Another Terrorist Against Terrorism

"I admire the strong leadership of President Musharraf."
—GW, State of the Union Address, 2003

Buffalo Bill Goes To Washington

"Dead or Alive."
—GW, on how he wanted Bin Laden

That's Not In The Job Description, GW

"I looked the man in the eye . . . I was able to get a sense of his soul."
—GW on Vladimir Putin

Rhetoric to Soothe Muslims By

"This CRUSADE, this war on terrorism is going to take a while."
—GW on the war on Afghanistan

More Soothing Words for Muslims . . .

[A] "pretty good political handbook."
—GW on the Bible

KING GEORGE CONFRONTS THE ENEMY

Rove: A bit of bad news, sir. The poll numbers are dropping again.

Bush: I thought you told me high ratings were guaranteed if I started a war.

Rove: Sorry, but a lot of people just aren't convinced you've shown any reason to attack Iraq.

Bush: Damn those peaceniks!

Rove: Actually, it's Admiral Shanahan and General Zinni and a lot of the intelligence community. They've taken out an ad in the newspaper criticizing your war policy. They say it will destabilize the Middle East, increase terrorism, incite blowback on the US, and waste resources essential to the American economy.

Bush: Oh, pick, pick pick! All they ever do is criticize.

OUR SHINING EXAMPLE

SEIZING THE MORAL HIGH GROUND

> *"He [Saddam Hussein] has gassed many Iranians, and 40 Iraqi villages."*
> —President Bush, September 12, 2002, UN General Assembly, New York City

He gassed his own people. Well, actually they were Kurds, but it sounds a lot worse if you say "his own people," so let's just do that even if it isn't true.

Of course, the US fully supported Hussein during the gassing but that doesn't mean we're evil, only Saddam. And just because the US provided satellite data for the gassing of Iran and continued delivering military assistance to Hussein even after the attack doesn't mean we are implicated in that act either, not at all. And so what if Middle East envoy Donald Rumsfeld shook Hussein's hand and tended to his needs after the heinous deeds were done? After all, what's a little gassing between friends?

But you'd be surprised how unfair people can be about this. A 1988 Senate Foreign Relations Committee investigation concluded that the US role in the gassing of Iran had emboldened Saddam to gas the Kurds at home. Committee Chair Claiborne Pell actually condemned the American silence "while people are gassed," calling it complicity and likening it to the world-wide hush that attended Hitler's extermination of the Jews. Hey, lighten up, dude!

Naturally, President Reagan opposed punishing Iraq with sanctions, preferring to reward Hussein with agricultural credits and deadly bacteria for his biological weapons program, which just goes to show you that compassionate conservatism wasn't born yesterday.

Alls well that ends well, so the media took its cue. When ABC correspondent Charles Glass revealed the site of one of Hussein's biological warfare programs ten months after the gassing of the Kurds at Halabja, Reagan's State Department denied the facts and the media dismissed the story because, well, it just wasn't newsworthy.

Inexplicably, it became newsworthy again when Washington decided to convert the entire Middle East to an American protectorate and needed a base country from which to

launch its takeover of the region. All of a sudden a gassing that had occurred well over a decade previously with full US backing became morally repugnant.

Demonizing Saddam over the acts it originally supported, the US invaded the country, took over the oil fields, and "liberated" the Iraqis, who kept shouting "Death to America" and committing suicide bombings against us for some peculiar reason. The ingratitude of some people is just too much!

Truman nuked his own people!

I am at a loss to explain why this never makes it into school textbooks, as it just fills me with pride. Ten days before Nagasaki was leveled by an atomic bomb the War Department received a message from Headquarters, US Army Strategic Air Forces, Guam, indicating that an Allied prisoner of war camp was situated one mile north of the city. The message requested an immediate reply as far as whether this affected plans to nuke the city. The reply stated that, "Targets previously assigned . . . remain unchanged." Martin Sherwin in his book _A World Destroyed_, concludes that American POWs were probably wiped out in the attack. Now if that doesn't prove the goodness of America I don't know what will. We even nuke our own to achieve peace. Is there any country more self-sacrificing than ours?

Four American presidents irradiated their own people!

Truman, Eisenhower, and JFK exposed hundreds of thousands of American soldiers and surrounding civilian populations to radioactive fallout from nuclear testing in the Nevada and Utah desert. The soldiers were told the fallout was harmless, which made sense given the quick and painless recovery of the Hiroshima and Nagasaki survivors. The Army encouraged its radiated conscripts to brush each other off with brooms in order to remove the completely non-dangerous radioactive particles clinging to their uniforms. The fact that these men later developed a lot of tumors means that they were genetically predisposed to suffer this fate, i.e. they had weak genes. So the Army was perfectly right in refusing all responsibility for their plight. But you'd be surprised how hard it was to convince the men of this. A lot of them insisted the Army pay for their medical bills. The damn spongers developed a crackpot conspiracy theory alleging that the Army had given them cancer by placing them in the path of nuclear fallout. Can you believe the lengths some people will go to to get a government dole? Shameful!

During the Gulf War, Bush the Elder spread radioactive contaminants all over the place when the US blew up two live nuclear reactors in Iraq. Of course, this has absolutely nothing to do with Gulf War Syndrome.

The US gassed and chemicalized its own troops!

Beginning in the early 1960s, the US showered South Vietnam and parts of Laos and Cambodia with thousands of tons of herbicides. Agent Orange was also widely used, but it's only 100,000 times more potent than Thalidomide, so it's nothing to lose sleep over. While it did cause some cancer and birth defects among the Vietnamese, we have to remember that they deserved this for opposing our demolition of their country. On the other hand, the cancer and genetic damage inflicted on American soldiers was a regrettable, if totally understandable incident, and rendered them tragic secondary victims of the noble Vietnam crusade. The primary victims, of course, were the war planners in Washington, who suffered a loss of "credibility" in launching further wars of annihilation due to the US being forced to leave the country. There's no telling how many vital wars we were inhibited from launching due to this loss of imperial dignity. This is clearly the most heartbreaking result of the war, though it rarely gets proper attention given everyone's fascination with trivialities like millions killed and three countries wrecked beyond repair.

The US Army also utilized CS, DM and CN gasses in Vietnam, although Washington sensibly insisted this was not "gas warfare" but "riot control." The Army pumped CS gas —a violent purgative inducing uncontrollable vomiting—into Vietnamese tunnels and caves, leaving victims choking to death in their own vomit in the cramped spaces, many of them women and children, not that it matters. Other happy effects included blistered faces, destroyed eyeballs, and scorched and erupted skin. US Deputy Secretary Cyrus Vance admitted that arsenic and cyanide were also being used. Other instruments favored by US forces were napalm and Naphthalene flame throwers.

Except for the poisoning of the American troops, though, none of this is of the slightest importance because the victims were not rich, white, or American. Sorry for bringing it up at all.

The Pentagon gassed its own troops!

From the 1940s to 1990s in Panama the US tested all kinds of chemical agents on mines, rockets, and shells, including mustard gas, VX, sarin, hydrogen cyanide, and other nerve agents. In the earlier years some troops were used as guinea pigs, with horrifying, but wonderfully patriotic results for the soldiers, who were glad to be of service.

The Pentagon and CIA practiced germ warfare on their own people!

In 1956 and 1958 the US Army unleashed swarms of specially bred mosquitos on Georgians and Floridians to test their usefulness for biological war. The mosquitos bred for the tests were of the Aedes Aegypti type, the carrier for dengue fever and other diseases.

For two decades the DoD and the CIA exposed millions of Americans to clouds of bacteria and chemicals in a series of open air tests.

In 1950 in the Watertown, New York area and the Virgin Islands, the Army dropped turkey feathers laced with cereal rust spores to poison oat crops, in order to establish that a "cereal rust epidemic" could be used as a biological weapon. Take my word for it, the unwitting subjects were more than happy to be part of the making of this determination.

From June 6-10, 1966, the Army loosed trillions of *Bacillus subtilus variant niger* in the New York City subway system during rush hour. Light bulbs full of the bacteria were furtively shattered at sidewalk level on subway ventilating grills or thrown on the roadbeds inside the stations. The air current from passing trains spread the bacteria far and wide. No follow up tests were needed because the government was acting in defense of the country, which is automatically good for Americans, even if it kills them.

For decades following WWII, the US government experimented on millions of human subjects, trying to gauge the effects of various nuclear, chemical, and biological agents, including nerve agents, ionizing radiation, plutonium injections, and mind-control drugs like SD and other hallucinogens and chemical cocktails. This is truly what love of country is all about.

In short, we've poisoned cities, laced the heavens with a *potpourri* of radiactive isotopes, showered regions with Agent Orange, and blown up live nuclear reactors. Therefore, we must demonstrate total respect to President Bush as he lectures the world on the depraved plans of "evildoers" out to destroy America with weapons of mass destruction.

WE SHALL MEET THEM IN THE MALLS, WE WILL MEET THEM ON THE CAR LOTS, WE SHALL NOT FALTER

King George and his royal court were quick to solve the problem of terrorists flying planes into our buildings because they hated our elected bicameral legislature. New York Mayor Rudolph Giuliani called for "the best shoppers in the world" to converge on restaurants, Broadway shows, and shops for a patriotic spending spree. President Bush recommended the terrorists be smashed with tourism. In a September 27, 2001 speech to airline employees at O'Hare International Airport, he said: "Get on the airlines, get about the business of America . . . Fly and enjoy America's great destination spots. Get down to Disney World in Florida. Take your families and enjoy life, the way we want it to be enjoyed." Jeb Bush's Florida officials hyped a "Freedom Weekend" devoted to spending money. Miami-Dade County Mayor Alex Panelas urged one and all to "Go out and contribute to the economy," quickly adding his wife's view that it had "never been more patriotic to go shopping."

Such were the awesome sacrifices demanded of us as we embarked on what the Bush Administration called "World War Three."

No doubt Osama bin Laden and Mullah Omar were cringing in their caves while our cash registers sang and our credit cards maxed out. Osama's rumored fatal illness was probably just the ebbing away of all desire for life following his failure to end consumerism as we know it.

I don't mind telling you that I was deeply grateful for official reminders of our sacred duty to consume, coming as they did with rescue workers sifting through a canyon of rubble in search of victims and parts of victims. It was obviously crucial to make sure that the incineration of thousands of innocent Americans hadn't made consumerism seem pointless, absurd, downright tasteless. Once people start thinking that way, the life of a rat race seems all too much like the life of a rat race. Thank God we got right back on track!

And congratulations to King George for explaining the new and improved spendthrift patriotism. Who can disagree with his profound insight that nothing should change now that everything has completely changed? If we allowed anything to change, especially the compulsive shopping that is our most endearing national trait, not to mention the economic bedrock of the greatest way of life ever devised, that would mean that the terrorists had won, had prevented us from returning to "normalcy," which is different from normality, don't ask me how.

And we can easily verify that nothing has changed by noting the comforting fact that we are still bombing the crap out of one country after another, just as we always have. So as JFK would say, ask not, "Why do they hate us?" but rather, "why don't we hate them more?" That's the way to keep the liberation bombs falling and consumption rising, which is what America is all about.

If you find any of this confusing, just remember that when proposals are made to push Pentagon budgets into the stratosphere and abolish the Bill of Rights it's because everything is different now and we can't indulge obsolete "September 10th" thinking anymore. But when the economy tanks because people are too terrified to consume as gluttonously as saturation advertising normally induces them to, then it becomes imperative to show that nothing is different at all, which can only be done by spending ourselves into oblivion.

Everything is different now, so we have to keep everything the same. Got it?

Full speed ahead then with blindly following our leaders, shipping our children off to die in remote corners of the world, and hitting the malls morning, noon, and night. While we're at it, let's put a lid on belly-aching about millions of lost jobs, pensions, homes, and all resistance to the idea of blowing our brains out, not to mention wondering what happened to the satellite-confirmed WMD Saddam supposedly had. Those are thoughts all too obviously reflective of an anachronistic pre-9/11 outlook, if not outright treason.

So everybody pull together and applaud the president's permanent war and fiscal train wreck, now ushering in record deficits that portend the end of Social Security and Medicare. History shows that a completely unregulated market brings abundance to all, so go ahead and spend away, even if your pension has been drained by corporate predators and your job has relocated to Indonesia and your family is in the street, not that there's anything wrong with any of that.

Well, I'm off to do my part. Now where's that damn shopping list? Oh, here it is: "Cipro, gas mask, automatic rifle, anthrax detection kit, geiger counter, duct tape, plastic sheeting . . ."

CHAPTER EIGHT

GENERAL ASHCROFT GOES TO WAR

ONE NATION UNDER SURVEILLANCE

SAFETY BUSH STYLE

"If this were a dictatorship, it would be a heck of a lot easier, just so long as I'm the dictator."

—GW Bush, December 18, 2000

Well, you can't say Bush isn't doing his best to deliver on this one. In the blink of an eye we've upgraded our democracy to include torture and secret tribunals and lifetime detention without trial and warrantless searches and expanded wiretapping and snooping on e-mail and monitoring client-counsel communications and giving library records to the

FBI and using face recognition technology to scan crowds for "evildoers" and spying on everyone "suspicious" and constructing a grand database to record every American's credit card transactions, bank and medical records, travel information, and phone calls, not to mention one-nation-under-God-with-digital-fingerprints-for-all under the wise guidance of former Navy Rear Admiral John Poindexter of Iran-Contra fame. It's also extremely comforting to know that we now have a Department of Homeland Security that will not be subject to Congressional or judicial oversight or pesky Freedom of Information Act requests.

Meanwhile, we are constantly warned of impending spectacular terrorist attacks as American troops move through a Middle East boiling over with anti-American resentments. I feel safer than ever, don't you?

HELP GEORGE STOP EVIL BEFORE IT STARTS

Inspired by King George's preventive war doctrine, Gore Vidal has explained the vital necessity of dispatching Mormon boys to concentration camps in order to end polygamy. We know they are going to practice it, so we simply must stop it in advance.

This stunningly brilliant "ounce of prevention" doctrine must be extended to save us from every variety of identity crime. For example, males are the cause of rape so all male babies must be castrated forthwith. This will also solve the circumcision controversy, eliminate the need for abortion, and make a big dent in the spread of VD.

A huge portion of our illegal immigration problem is caused by Mexicans and Central Americans. Therefore, we must start above-ground nuclear testing in these regions right away. No more Mr. Nice Guy.

Corporate accounting scandals are caused by rich white men. Therefore, we have to sterilize these men immediately and kill any children they may already have. The child-killings and mass vasectomies should be nationally televised to deter the ascendancy of middle class whites, who are racially and culturally suspect and therefore probably carriers of the corruption virus.

POLICE VIDEO CAMERAS PLACED AT INTERSECTIONS CUT DOWN ON TRAFFIC VIOLATIONS. THIS SUCCESS LEADS AMERICANS TO EMBRACE THIS EXCITING TECHNOLOGY AT HOME...

A SMALL INCONVENIENCE FOR SO MUCH LAW AND ORDER!

Good Citizen Cam
GET YOURS TODAY!

Racism can be prevented by genetically engineering human beings to have identical racial characteristics, i.e. Caucasian. Non-whites who can't afford designer babies should simply bleach the color out of their skin.

An obvious means of preventing ethnic conflicts is to raise test tube babies right in the labs. No culture, no conflict. Problem solved.

If all of this is giving you a headache, you might consider King George's lifetime headache cure—decapitation. Book an appointment with the Department of Homeland Security right away.

HOMELAND SECURITY SELF - EXAM

TO BE DONE ONCE WEEKLY!

PATRIOGRAM

To reduce the number of Patriograms™ done in our office we've developed this quick and easy self-exam

JUST ASK YOURSELF THESE 3 QUESTIONS...

Who is the Evil-Doer?

 A.)

 B.)

 C.)

We are attacked by terrorists. Your response is:

A) cut taxes and start a war!

B) Praise Allah!

C) Why do they hate us?

You use your sneakers for:
A). tennis
B). explosives
C.) demonstrating

If "A" was not your answer to each of the above turn yourself in - immediately

M. WUERKER

TOTAL SAFETY THROUGH TOTAL POLICE POWER

President Bush is a genius.

Think about it. What makes the terrorists hate us? Our freedom. So if we destroy the freedoms embodied in our Constitution the terrorists will stop hating us and our security will be assured.

In fact, President Bush's insightful November 13, 2001 order authorizing the creation of secret military tribunals is probably steadily winning Al Qaeda over with its irresistible charm. The President alone now gets to decide what type of actions have "an adverse effect on the United States, its citizens, national security, foreign policy, or economy." And no matter how much these words may seem to implicate his own policies you can count on President Bush not to notice. Instead, he or anyone he designates will lord unlimited power over those they choose to regard as enemies, simultaneously acting as rule-maker, investigator, accuser, prosecutor, judge, jury, sentencing court, reviewing court, jailer, and executioner. Now that's the kind of multi-tasking that gets positive results!

And there is absolutely no danger to our civil liberties. The only people who have to worry about being seized and brought before a military tribunal are those whom the President suspects are: (1) members of Al Qaeda; (2) somehow involved in "acts of international terrorism"; (3) "knowingly harbor[ing]" persons in either of the first two categories. Happily, no definition of "Al Qaeda" or "international terrorism" is offered, so the President is free to make law at will, banning behavior on a whim and changing his mind every other day if he likes. Since no one can know in advance what behavior to avoid, everyone will be afraid, which means that we will have no freedom, which means Al Qaeda won't hate us anymore, which means we'll be safe.

A swell bonus is that preventive detention and clandestine execution now become the basis of policework. The Bush order allows us to dispense with probable cause and the neurotic obsession over whether or not a crime has been committed, because terrorism is a crime of motivation, not an overt act. Thus, our intention, not our behavior, is what President Bush and Attorney General Ashcroft must judge, and if these two righteous Christians have any inkling that one of us is up to something evil they are fully empowered to have us seized, tried, and executed, which makes me feel a lot safer just thinking about it.

Furthermore, since there is no judicial review of charges, the President needn't ever justify his feeling that a given suspect is guilty of evil intentions. Someone who provided housing years ago to someone who later is labeled a terrorist can be dragged before a secret tribunal and eliminated under the wonderfully elastic "harboring terrorists" formula.

THOUGHT CRIMES
GEORGE BUSH IS AN IMBECILE AND AN ILLEGITIMATE PRESIDENT.
WAR IS NOT THE ANSWER
No, I don't support the troops going into Iraq ...or Syria or..
Maybe, just maybe, there are people in the world who don't want to live like Americans.
FOUR THOUGHTS YOU CAN'T HAVE ANYMORE
M. WUERKER

How much more secure can we get?

Tribunal rules of procedure are in the able hands of the Secretary of Defense, who has sole power to determine the scope of protections afforded the accused. There's nothing to worry about here because Donald Rumsfeld is eminently fair-minded. When asked before the Iraq War what it would prove if weapons inspectors found no WMD, he responded, "What it would prove would be that the inspection process had been successfully defeated by the Iraqis." Guilty even if proven innocent, now that's just the man for judicial work!

If the backlog of terrorism cases becomes a great burden, the accused can rot in jail forever without being charged or given a trial date, since there are no time limits specified in the Bush order. If evidence is lacking for conviction, hearsay is perfectly admissable, which is a shot in the arm to stool pigeons, who now have plenty of opportunity to wreck people for personal reasons with no fear of consequences. Since the accused have no right to face their accusers, testimony can be orchestrated by the state and received in secret in order to guarantee conviction and protect "national security."

Torture is acceptable, if not downright necessary, and testimony in the form of extracted confessions, unsworn statements and unauthenticated reports are perfectly valid evidence. We can't wait for a smoking gun—we're dealing with evildoers here.

All of the key roles in the military tribunals are to be filled by military officers designated by the President. One group of military officers will present evidence to another group of military officers, and all the officers will, of course, report to the President as Commander-in-Chief. Defense counsel will also be a military officer, one whom the defendant will have no right to dismiss. If a civilian defense attorney is used, he or she will not be allowed to be present during any part of the tribunal proceeding that is ordered closed by the Presiding Officer or the President, and the military officer appointed as defense counsel will be in overall charge of the defense.

Juries are obsolete, as suspects will be tried by three to seven members of the US armed forces. Public trials are out, as proceedings will be open only at the discretion of the President or the Secretary of Defense. Double jeopardy is in, because defendants acquitted in civilian federal court may be retried before a military tribunal for the same offense, where rules of evidence need not prevail. Best of all, a two-thirds vote of military officers authorizes execution.

Defendants need not be presented with charges in a language they understand and there is no guarantee that an interpreter will be present. The proceedings of the tribunal may be kept secret even from the accused, who can be excluded for national security reasons. Classified information is to remain secret at all times, even if it is the sole evidence brought against a defendant and the defendant never gets to examine it.

Convictions and sentences of the military tribunal, including life imprisonment or death, can be reviewed only by the same officials who brought charges. Fortunately, we live in a society where those who wield total power are honorable, trustworthy men who readily own up to their mistakes. See the Economic Hall of Fame for evidence of this boundless integrity.

The long and short of it is that individuals can be arrested, held without charge, tried in secret by the Pentagon, denied opportunity to question the evidence, convicted by a two-thirds vote, sentenced to death, and executed, all without Congress, the public, or the judiciary ever knowing anything about it.

By the time we get this new justice system in high gear, Al Qaeda will love us.

SECRET TRIALS HERALD BRIGHT FUTURE

BUSH CITES PERMANENT 'EMERGENCY'

By Debra Dimwit
The Lapdog Ledger

Declaring his 64th "extraordinary emergency" in two weeks, President Bush yesterday ordered military trials for suspected international terrorists, disloyal journalists, anti-war protestors, and anyone ordering French fries or engaging in a passionate kiss.

Administration officials explained that the purpose of the military tribunals is to ensure that treasonous beliefs are brought swiftly and surely to an end, as required by the national security clause of the Constitution.

The president said the tribunals are necessary because "mass deaths, mass injuries and massive destruction of property" caused by terrorists could impede ongoing US efforts to inflict "mass deaths, mass injuries and massive destruction of property" on evildoers. Fielding complaints from Amnesty International

about tossing out "principles of law and rules of evidence," Bush said that these are "irrelevant" when pursuing "the bad guys."

The president's decision is the latest in a series of legal steps taken by the government to combat terrorism. Last week, the Justice Department authorized jailing defense lawyers along with their clients, denouncing them as "evil." Congress has also passed legislation making it illegal to manufacture phones without a built-in wiretap. House Majority Leader Tom Delay complained that, "It is inconceivable that there are still untapped phones in the United States in the 21st Century," which he insisted was "an insult to the FBI."

Legal scholars declaring the measure of dubious validity were not available for comment. Colleagues indicated they had "vanished without a trace" right after lunch with Attorney General Ashcroft.

© 2003 The Lapdog Ledger

TAX CUTS BREED MORE PATRIOTIC AMERICA

King George's fiscal wisdom has already done much to make America a better place. Among the benefits trickling down from his trillions of dollars in tax cuts is the can-do inventiveness of the parents and teachers at the Family School in Eugene Oregon. With the school facing a fierce budget crunch parent Lorrie Burns came up with the idea to have the parents and teachers sell their blood plasma to keep the school going. When she presented her proposal to a community meeting the crowd burst into applause.

So Aventis Bio-Services in Eugene was brought in to perform this breakthrough in education funding. Aventix manager Alf Moebius pronounced the plan a "win-win situation," not to mention another splendid example of public-private partnership. By all accounts the event was a grand success, although one parent was inexplicably short on enthusiasm for the momentous achievement: "It's a bizarre and poignant place we've come to, when we're reduced to donating our bodily fluids to support our schools. It's definitely our last stand."

But there's no reason it has to be. With state governments already bankrupt and more huge tax cuts for the rich bringing $500 billion deficits into view, I think it is safe to say that the opportunity to "think outside the box" like the parents at the Family School will present itself again and again.

So let's make a virtue of necessity and try to come up with more real solutions to tough budget problems. How about extracting just a bit more from our bodies? Citizens could offer up spare kidneys to keep Medicare afloat, that extra eye for Social Security. And if enough people gave up some of their bone marrow for the new Missile Defense System we could give the corporations yet another big tax cut. King George could urge us to "leave no unharvested body behind." Religious leaders could remind us that the body is God's temple, though something would surely have to be done about the gooey donations to the collection plate.

As a counter to militant Islam's suicide bombers, we could develop suicide donors, patriots who literally give their all for school supplies. On Memorial Days we could honor them. "Here lies John Doe, fiscal patriot. His brave last words were: 'I regret that I have but one liver to give to the high school music program.'"

CHAPTER NINE

TO SUM UP....

The Seven Habits of Highly Effective Empires

1) Weave Big Myths.

Myths make Empire's violent subjugations seem like tender solicitude. In India the British taught not only English literature, but the superiority of the "race" that produced it. As we instruct Iraqis in the gentle art of self-government-without-kicking-us-out, we can impart the wisdom that conquest reflects our innate moral superiority. They're sure to love us for that.

If things fall apart, the ever-popular "civilized race besieged by ungrateful barbarians" theme works wonders. The British blamed climate and geography for Indians being "inherently untruthful and lack[ing] moral courage." Lord Cromer, the virtual ruler of Egypt from 1883 to 1906, asserted that "Orientals" didn't have it in them to learn to walk on sidewalks, tell the truth, or employ logic. The best bet for the USA is to blame corrupt sheiks, ignorant "camel jockeys," and prehistoric "sand niggers" for squandering our gift of liberation.

2) Merge Business and the State.

World domination requires exclusive trading privileges and massive applications of force. The brigands who laid the foundation for European merchant empires of the 17th and 18th centuries fused war with trade and unleashed flocks of warrior-merchants on an unsuspecting world. Generations of region-ravaging wars, mass poverty, and monopoly profits were the happy results. According to Adam Smith, the British converted Bengal from a rich land to a place where "three or four hundred thousand people die of hunger in one year." One of their methods was replacing rich fields of grain with opium poppies.

King George and Co. carry on this venerable imperial tradition. No one knows where Halliburton ends and the Pentagon begins as Dick Cheney selflessly flits from Secretary of Defense to CEO of Halliburton to Vice-President of the World. Firms that bankrolled Bush's near-election in 2000 land huge construction contracts while Iraqi masses see their basic services collapse and hear the UN chief of mission warn of humanitarian disaster.

Not to worry. Imperial memory is short. Starving Afghans are already forgotten now that GW has handled the important task: handing the country over to a Unocal consult-ant to negotiate a natural gas pipeline through the country. Prosperity for all is on the way!

3) Get Others to do the Dying.

Ancient Rome fought to the "last Aetoli," the pre-WWII British to "the last Frenchman." Ninety percent of the forces holding India for Britain were native merce-naries. Washington also prefers proxies, primarily denationalized looters and their frisky security forces, who guarantee a "favorable investment climate" of cheap labor, no unions or regulations, generous profit repatriation, and low taxes. Mountains of corpses result, but none are American, so we don't need to count them.

Nevertheless, Lord Wolfowitz contends it is unwise to rely on client regimes, so now we're back to direct colonial administration.

Just keep repeating, "We're here to liberate," and ignore the thunderous cries of "Death to America!"

4] Forget the Past.

Memory is inconvenient to Empire, which is fun to acquire but impossible to hold. Amnesia is the road to renewal.

So forget the enormous losses of life and property and the painful decline of Empires past. Forget that Indonesia pulled away from Holland, Britain handed India back to the Congress Party, and Malaysia, Ceylon and Burma broke free of the imperial yoke. Forget the ruinous French-Algerian wars and Washington's quasi-genocidal lark in Southeast Asia. Forget the dozens of new African states and how they came about. And definitely forget the mounds of Filipino corpses that troubled Mark Twain and the look of burning hatred in Hawaiian eyes.

The sun never sets on the American Empire. Long live Baghdad, USA.!

5] Be Racist.

If you're going to rob people blind, it's best to develop a bad image of them first to make the going easier. Thus, Empire-builders love talk of bringing civilization to savages, wild aborigines, "natives," lower orders, lesser breeds, and "backward" countries. Such non-white peoples are always and everywhere "lazy," "stupid," and "unreliable." E. S. Grogan, who traversed the African continent at the end of the 19th century, found Africans "but slightly superior to the lower animals." Sir Rudolph Slatin in the Sudan detected a flaw in African economic relations: "The nigger is a lazy beast and must be compelled to work."

American leaders have been just as insightful. Loss of racial purity alarmed Thomas Jefferson, who wanted to ship the blacks to Africa or the Caribbean, leaving the USA without "blot or mixture." A century later, Woodrow Wilson was screening the Klan-friendly "Birth of a Nation" at the White House and the United States occupied Haiti (1915-1934). In charge of the invasion was General Smedley Butler, who found the locals to be, "shaved apes, absolutely no intelligence whatsoever, just plain low nigger."

Beloved Teddy Roosevelt thought the Nazi-like Sand Creek massacre of 1864 (Colorado) was "righteous and beneficial," eagerly charged up San Juan Hill (Kettle Hill for you purists) to "whip the dagos" in 1898, and disdained the "Malay bandits" and "Chinese halfbreeds" resisting US conquest of the Philippines. These Filipinos he rated no better than "savages, barbarians, a wild and ignorant people, Apaches, Sioux, Chinese boxers." He's a hero. Check with Mt. Rushmore.

As he immolated Southeast Asia, Richard Nixon peppered his private conversations with references to "niggers," "jigaboos," and "jungle bunnies." He instructed Henry Kissinger to make sure his first foreign policy message to Congress had "something in it for the jigs."

The Baby Boomer presidents have toned down the racist rhetoric while continuing to rain death on non-white peoples from the Imperial Sky. I guess they don't want to hurt anyone's feelings.

6) Invent Self-Serving Euphemisms.

The Founding Fathers understood the importance of Empire. They openly spoke of the need to kill Indians, to guide slaves from savagery to civilization, to conquer and subdue foreign lands under an American banner. They and succeeding generations of American rulers regarded it as their privilege and duty to rob, swindle, torture, and murder all those who obstructed their onward march to the materialist paradise. As a result, the Indians were destroyed, generations of slaves were worked to death, half of Mexico was captured by drunken invaders, Spain's colonies were seized, and American power circled the globe.

This was variously called "extending the area of freedom," maintaining "territorial and administrative integrity," and "saving the world for democracy."

7) Keep Expanding.

"The history of the nation is in large part the history of the nation's expansion," said Teddy Roosevelt, which goes to show that the current fashion of attributing American Empire to a virgin birth in the era of King George is hardly fair.

Expansion inspired George Washington to offer intriguing anthropological speculations. In 1783 he wrote that "the gradual extension of our settlements will as certainly cause the savage, as the wolf, to retire; both being beasts of prey, tho' they differ in shape." Thomas Jefferson found Indian peoples "backward" and foresaw that with expansion "we shall be obliged to drive them, with the beasts of the forests into the Stony mountains." He fully intended to take Canada along the way.

Chief Justice John Marshall came up with legal justification for Indian removal—"discovery." Simply declaring the land "discovered," he said, "gave an exclusive right to extinguish the Indian right of occupancy."

Now King George, that sly fox, has "discovered" the oil fields of Central Asia and Iraq. He's such a traditionalist!

APPENDIX

SORTING OUT THE PROPAGANDA

BUSHEVIK IDEOLOGY - A GLOSSARY OF TERMS

accountability, n. - conformity, submission. Only demanded of those spending government money for public health, education, or welfare. No accountability is requested or required of those who allocate of billions of taxpayer dollars to a Star Wars defense shield that has failed repeated tests. But rat infested schools with leaky roofs must be held accountable for the lavish sums they receive, lest educators figure out a way to remedy such conditions. See also *humiliation*.

achievement gap, n. - a structured "educational" outcome derived from class division. In a class divided society, whatever the rich do is achievement and whatever the poor do is failure. That is, since the poor are clearly not rich, they are deficient. Hence the "achievement gap." See also *gap of hope*.

alert citizens, n. - spies. See also *armies of compassion*.

American Dream, n. - limitless consumption. Example: *Five minutes after the president announced the broadest achievement of the American Dream in history, human beings went extinct.* See also *ecocide*.

American values, n. - the flag, the national anthem, and Church. Example: *The bombing of the orphanage was carried out with due respect for American values.*

armies of compassion, n. - Christian missionaries. This group is allegedly so numerous and generous that social welfare programs are obsolete. Example: *President Bush's armies of compassion delivered thousands of American evildoers to the secret tribunals today.*

axis of evil, n. - two mortal enemies and an economic basket case.

budget crisis, n. - an ideological construct designed to convince the victims of a robbery that they must pay back the money that has been stolen from them.

choice, n. - coercion. Example: *The elimination of alternatives to the corporate order is essential to maintaining choice.*

compassionate coercion, n. - forcing people to accept Jesus before they may receive government assistance for drug addiction, homelessness etc.

core values, n. - entrenched dogmas.

cycle of dependency, n. - an affliction of the poor, who make a habit of eating and are strangely reluctant to give it up. Example: *After the government withdrew from the public housing market, hundreds of thousands of Americans escaped their cycle of dependency in preference for living in the Great Outdoors.*

deliver a message, v. launch a military attack. Example: *The Enola Gay delivered a message to the people of Japan.*

dignity, n. - unrestrained egoism, arrogance.

discipline, n. - a quality much lacking in the poor but which can be readily instilled by tossing them to the wolves.

ecocide, n. - the basis of "growing the economy."

educational entrepreneurs, n. - entrepreneurs. Example: *The educational entrepreneurs improved the efficiency of the schools by closing them down.*

efficiency, n. a mystical notion holding that gluttonous excess on all fronts represents the most prudent use of resources.

entitlement, n. - the scourge of the modern era. A belief of lazy people that they deserve to be compensated sufficiently to live a decent life, whether or not they are skilled at prostituting themselves to the rich. Civilization will grind to a halt if this notion becomes a majority sentiment. See also *budget crisis*.

equality, n. a highly unnatural state desired only by Communists and madmen. In the eyes of God the condition is purely metaphysical, which is how it should remain.

family, n. - a faith-based organization in which Dad dominates, Mom procreates, and the kids vegetate.

firmness, n.- ideological rigidity, a great virtue. Example: *The president's firmness on the need to Americanize the world led to nuclear war.*

freedom, n. - the right to waste. See *overconsumption*.

friends and allies, n. - the bought and the blackmailed. Example: *The invasion of Iraq was backed by a broad coalition of friends and allies like Eritrea, Micronesia, and Uzbekistan.*

gap of hope, n. - the failure of the urban poor to adopt the cheerful optimism of those who live by exploiting them. Says King George in his book "A Charge To Keep": *"They do not believe the fundamentally American conviction that you can be what you want to be, and achieve what you want to achieve . . ."* (p. 227) Indeed. Unfortunately, his Royal Highness provides no evidence to dissuade them from this quite reasonable conclusion. See also *achievement gap.*

greatness of America, n. - the overwhelming dominance of American military and financial power on the world scene. Example: *Attacking Iraq with a space-age arsenal after forcing it to disarm shows the greatness of America.*

high-standards, n. - what the rich have and the poor desperately need.

humiliation, n. - what there is never enough of. The glue that binds the GOP together. See also *dignity.*

international law, n. - when it accords with US foreign policy objectives, a redundancy; when it deviates, an irrelevance.

keep the peace, v. - to endlessly expand the permanent war economy and maintain American supremacy no matter how many countries are destroyed in the process.

justice, n. - at home: capital punishment; abroad: massive bombardment with missiles and bombs.

liberate, v. - to enslave under new management.

limited government, n. - a police state with a Mickey Mouse facade.

overconsumption, n. - a logical impossibility.

peace, n. - a nanosecond between violent subjugations.

personal responsibility, n. - abstention from out-of-wedlock sex.

private sector alternatives, n. - the engine of public sector impoverishment. Example: *Hiring a limousine instead of getting to work by bus is one of the private sector alternatives that makes America great.*

raising the bar, n. - reducing access to essential resources. Guaranteeing that more people fall short of "high standards" so less money need be spent on them.

rebuild American military power, v. - to accelerate the ongoing build-up of US military power.

responsibility era, n. - a time when Norman Vincent Peale will look like a skeptic.

returning money to the taxpayers, v. - rewarding the rich with tax relief in order to induce a budget crisis, which in turn can be exploited as a pretext to dismantle government programs that benefit the non-rich.

right, n. - (1) a refuge for criminals. (2) An arrogant and

entirely invalid claim against property interests. (3) according to John Ashcroft, a means of aiding and abetting terrorism.

sanctity of life, n. - fetal sovereignty.

security, n. - limitless, unaccountable authority. Example: *The president's policy of torturing political heretics bolstered American security.*

soft bigotry of low expectations, n. - the failure to impose the hard bigotry of "high standards" on the children of the poor.

solemn commitment, n. - empty promise.

something-for-nothing, n. - what the rich get, which causes them to fear that everyone wants it.

those less fortunate, n. - the pitilessly exploited.

tough realism, n. - fanatical idealism. Example: *When grandmother came up short on her rent money, the landlord gave her a lesson in tough realism by throwing her into the snow.*

unity, n. obedience.

A Swindler's Guide To "Creative Accounting"

abuses and excesses, n. - corporate robbery that achieves public notice, which is a breach of etiquette in ruling circles. The subtext is that the routine depredations of the market are legitimate. See also *fraud-and-scandal*.

accounting plan, n. - King George's remedy for the corporate accounting scandals. Consists of putting the criminals on the honor system.

acts of deception, high-profile n. - thievery on such a grand scale that even the most devoted media lapdogs can't cover it up.

ambition, n. - lust for gain, a virtue. Example: *Ken Lay was a man of considerable ambition.*

ask tough questions, v. - to feign indignation at corporate plundering until the public loses interest in the media hype, which rarely discloses that systemic inducements to massive fraud remain in place.

breaching the public trust, by CEOs, n. - financial gang rape that has allegedly gone too far, though there is no reason to suppose so.

build wealth, v. - deplete wealth; steal. Example: *Enron builds wealth by buying influence, plundering public assets, and gouging consumers..*

capitalism without conscience, n. - garden variety capitalism, allegedly correctable by "tough new laws."

compromised, adj. - open for business.

conflict of interest, n. - mutuality of interest. Example: *Andersen Accounting had a conflict of* *interest in collecting huge fees for helping Ken Lay rob his employees of their pension funds.*

corporate responsibility, n. - an oxymoron pleasing to the untrained ear.

cut ethical corners, v. - engage in wholesale looting. Example: *The fraudulent accounting reports were used to hype the company stock to undreamed of heights, which the CEO and his friends on the board of managers cashed in for billions of dollars just before the company went bankrupt. President Bush regretted the decision to cut ethical corners.*

deception, n. - a capitalist imperative that comes in two varieties, voluntary and involuntary. The poor practice involuntary deception in order to survive, which is taken as evidence of bad character. The rich are induced to practice voluntary deception via complex financial regulations, a process that coincidentally awards them huge profits.

destructive greed, n. - a redundancy. The supreme value under capitalism, which everyone is required to uphold. It becomes temporarily odious when scandals give it a bad name.

discipline federal spending, v. - cut programs that aid the general public.

economic slowdown, n. - collapse of public confidence in the financial system due to unrestrained fraud.

ethical compass, n. - a financial Boy Scout manual.

fraud-and-scandal, n.- a redundancy. Only the second word is operative. When undetected, fraud is a much admired and highly compensated skill in elite financial circles. Once detected, it is a temporary inconvenience.

fudge the numbers, v. - invent numbers out of whole cloth in order to defraud workers and investors. This characterization is roughly equivalent to accusing Heinrich Himmler of fudging on the Good Samaritan ethic.

higher ethical standards, n. - moral grandstanding that is allegedly the cure for gargantuan corporate rip-offs. Principles not to be acted upon. See also *moral showcase.*

honest advice, n. - a pack of lies, which is standard fare given capitalism's something-for-nothing ethic. Example: *After the company shill masquerading as a TV stock analyst gave the public some honest advice, billions of dollars in pension funds were liquidated as the company she had recommended plunged into bankruptcy.*

increase investor confidence, v. - move in for a repeat kill, bait.

integrity, new era of, on Wall Street, n. - one of the most treasured possessions of King George's imagination.

integrity of American business leaders, n. - the smallest particle in the known universe, undetected by the most powerful microscopes. Theoretical, like quarks.

job creation, n. - tax cuts for the rich.

momentum of our markets, n. - the precipitous decline that is leading us to a Golden Future.

moral confusion, n. - allegedly ambiguous financial norms that make corporate robbers sympathetic figures. It is identical to the moral relativism detested in liberals, but King George reserves considerable sympathy for it in the realm of financial affairs.

moral showcase, n. - a place to exhibit high principles never acted upon. In the era of King George it is jam-packed.

ENRON STATE PENN.

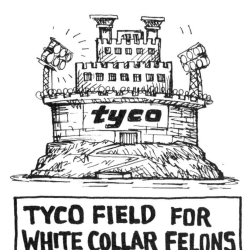

TYCO FIELD FOR WHITE COLLAR FELONS

promote transparency, v. - reduce the glare of temporary bad publicity so corporations can get back to inconspicuous methods of bilking the public.

bold, well-considered reforms, n. - hastily-drafted cosmetic changes.

regain the trust of, v. - sweet-talk, hoodwink. Example: *Seeking to regain the trust of the American people, the president explained that his tax cut for the rich would create prosperity for all.*

responsible business leaders, n. - an especially clever group of corporadoes able to combine high thievery with high public esteem.

root out corruption, v. - slap the wrists of a few small fry in order to protect the vast plunder secured by less conspicuous operations of the market.

sustained recovery, n. - the modern equivalent of Heaven, and seen just as often.

tax cut, n. - absolution for the obscenely rich. The reward for having been previously rewarded.

teamwork, n. - the common bond between the billionaire CEO and his unionless janitor.

terrorism insurance, n. - the ultimate protection racket, in which the public guarantees compensation to corporations in the event of losses caused by the terrorism their system is built upon.

tough laws, n. - a propaganda device designed to persuade the public that something is being done about the relentless pillage of public assets for private gain. Exhibit A in the president's moral showcase.

Endnotes

Introduction

George Carlin quoted from *Braindroppings*. p.206.
I am indebted to Michael parenti for the use of the term "King of the Planet" See his *The Terrorism Trap, September 11 and Beyond*
As for "Bushevik" Bush biographer JH Hatfield coined the term. See his *Fortunate Son, George W. Bush and the Making of an American President*

Chapter 1

Sources for Timeline:

J. H. Hatfield. *Fortunate Son - George W. Bush and the Making of an American President.*

George W. Bush. *A Charge To Keep.*

Elizabeth Mitchell. *W - Revenge of the Bush Dynasty.*

Christopher Simpson. *The Splendid Blonde Beast.*

Michael Lind. *Made In Texas: George W. Bush and The Southern Takeover of American Politics.*

Bill Minutaglio. *First Son - George W. Bush and the Bush Family Dynasty.*

Arianna Huffington. *Pigs At The Trough.*

Walter V. Robinson. One-year gap in Bush's National Guard duty. *Boston Globe*, 5/23/2000.

Bob Woodward. *Bush at War.*

Carolyn B. Thompson and James W. Ware, *The Leadership Genius of George W. Bush .*

William Rivers Pitt. *The Greatest Sedition is Silence - Four Years in America.*

Paul Slansky, *The Clothes Have No Emperor.*

Sources for Collected Wisdom:
Hatfield. *Fortunate Son.*
Thompson/Ware. *The Leadership Genius of George W. Bush.*

Chapter 2
Source for Count Dollars, Not Ballots:
Greg Palast. *The Best Democracy Money Can Buy,* Chapter 1.

Chapter 3

Sources on Dick Cheney: Cheney's voting record:
http://www.pbs.org/newshour/bb/politics/july-dec00/cheney_7-26.html
www.abcnews.go.com/sections/politics/DailyNews/Cheney_GMA000727.html
Cheney at the Helm. *The Progressive,* September 2000.
Noam Chomsky. *Deterring Democracy.*
Michael Parenti. *Democracy For The Few.*
Arianna Huffington. *Pigs At The Trough.*
Michael Lind. *Made in Texas,.*
Charles Lewis quoted on CBS *60 Minutes.* April 27, 2003.

Sources on Rumsfeld:
Phyllis Bennis. *Before & After - US Foreign Policy and the September 11th Crisis.*
Thomas R. Dye. *Who Rules America? - The Bush Restoration.*
Helen Caldicott. *The New Nuclear Danger - George W. Bush's Military Industrial Complex.*

Sources for Colin Powell:
Michael Moore. *Stupid White Men.*
Phyllis Bennis. *Before and After.*
William Blum. *Rogue State.*
Thomas R. Dye. *Who's Running America.*
Norman Solomon and Reese Erlich. *Target Iraq: What the News Don't Tell You.*
Michael Klare. *Rogue States and Nuclear Outlaws.*
Ramsey Clark. *The Fire This Time.*
Michael Parenti. Defying the Sanctions. *Z Magazine.* February 2001.
Web sources:
http://www.latimes.com/lawarpowell10apr10011417,0,5057419.story
http://www.pbs.org/itvs/enemiesofwar/timeline2.html

Sources for Condoleezza Rice:
Helen Caldicott. *The New Nuclear Danger - George W. Bush's Military Industrial Complex.*
Phyllis Bennis. *Before & After.*
Antonia Felix.*Condi.*

Norman Solomon. *Washington Journal*. October 15, 2001.

Reuters. "Chevron Oil Tanker Runs Aground Off Denmark." February 7, 2003.

Athen Manuel. The Dirty Four. *US Public Interest Research Group*, March 22, 2001.

Sources: for Paul Wolfowitz:
Edward Herman. Good and Bad Genocide. *EXTRA!* Sept./Oct. 1998.

Tim Shorrock. Paul Wolfowitz, Reagan's Man in Indonesia, Is Back at the Pentaton. *http://www.foreign policyinfocus.org/progresp/volume5/v5n10_body.html*

Caldicott cited from her book, *The New Nuclear Danger*.

Sources for Richard Perle:
Ronald Brownstein and Nina Easton. *Reagan's Ruling Class*.

Helen Caldicott. *The New Nuclear Danger*.

Perle quote on Hans Blix in Norman Solomon and Reese Erlich. *Target Iraq: What The News Media Didn't Tell You*.

Richard Perle, Thank God for the death of the UN, *Guardian*. March 21, 2003.

Source on Karl Rove:
Lou Dubose, Jan Reid, Carl M. Cannon. *Boy Genius - Karl Rove, the Brains Behind the Remarkable Political Triumph of George W. Bush*.

Sources on Ashcroft:
Michael Moore. *Stupid White Men*.

Thomas R. Dye. *Who's Running America? - The Bush Restoration*.

J. H. Hatfield. *Fortunate Son - George W. Bush and the Making of an American President*.

Bill Berkowitz. John Ashcroft: Attorney General from the Right. *Z Magazine*, February 2001.

FAIR. Attorney general nominee praised white supremacist magazine. *www.fair.org*

Ashcroft quoted in *Mother Jones*, Nov/Dec. 1998.

Sources for Tom Ridge
Linn Washington. Tom Ridge's record raises questions. 10-13-01 *www.progressive.org*

Stephen Moore. Veepstakes 2000, *National Review Online*, 7-21-00.

Thomas Frank. Ridge: Attack is 'Unlikely,' Keep Duct Tape In Storage. *Newsday*. 2-15-03.

Ridge, Speech to the National Press Club, April 29, 2003.

Sources on Gail Norton:
David Helvarg. Bushwhacked.www.metroactive.com

Michael Moore. *Stupid White Men*.

Douglas Jehl. Interior Choice Sends a Signal on Land Policy. *www.knowthecandidates.org*. December 30, 2000. *Democracy Now*. January 16, 2001.

James Ridgeway. *Village Voice*. January 30 - February 6, 2001. http://www.naacp.org/news/releases/gnorton01122001.s html

Sources for Elliot Abrams:
William Lutz. *Doublespeak*.

Noam Chomsky. *Turning The Tide - US Intervention in Central America and the Struggle for Peace*.

William Blum. *Killing Hope - US Military and C.I.A. Interventions Since World War II*.

Terry J. Allen. Public Serpent. www.InTheseTimes.com August 2001.

Abrams interviewed on Charlie Rose, March 31, 1995.

Sources for Otto Reich:
Phyllis Bennis. *Before & After*.

Noam Chomsky. *Chronicles of Dissent*.

http://www.foreignpolicyinfocus.org/republicanrule/officials_body.html#reich

Chapter 4

Source for "Gut Our Benefits":
Lee Sustar. They're Out To Gut Medicare. *Socialist Worker*. March 13, 2003.

Source for GW and the Environment:
Arianna Huffington. *Pigs At The Trough*.

Chapter 5

Sources for "How to Get Lay'd":
Greg Palast. *The Best Democracy Money Can Buy*.

Ian Hudson. *The Guardian*. November 6, 2002;

Sunday Observer, "Two men driving Bush into war" February 23, 2003.
Bernie Ward. KGO Radio. May 6, 2002.

Sources for "How To Get Screwed":
Bernie Ward, KGO Radio.May 6, 2002.
Greg Palast. *The Best Democracy Money Can Buy.*
Vijay Prashad. *Fat Cats and Running Dogs, The Enron Stage of Capitalism.*

Sources for Education (1) and (2):
Kevin D. Vinson and E. Wayne Ross. What We Can Know and When We Can Know It, *Z Magazine*. March 2001.
Stan Karp. Bush Plan Fails Schools. *Z Magazine*. April 2001.

Sources for "King George's Economic Hall of Fame":
Greg Eckler and L. M. MacDonald. *Bull! - 144 Stupid Statements From The Market's Fallen Prophets.*
Arianna Huffington. *Pigs At The Trough - How Corporate Greed and Political Corruption Are Undermining America.*
Alexander Cockburn. *Washington Babylon.*
Noam Chomsky. *The Umbrella of US Power - The Universal Declaration of Human Rights and the Contradictions of US Policy.*
Raymond Ker. Not Another World Con. *Z Magazine*. September 2002.

Source for Letter to Ken Lay:
Ken Lay quoted from Arianna Huffington's, *Pigs At The Trough.*

Chapter 6
Sources for Giving Africa the Business:
http://www.washingtonpost.com/ac2/wp-dyn?pagename=article&node=&contentId=A4784-2001Jun14&notFound=true)
America and Africa *Current History*. May 2003.
Africa Policy for a New Era: Ending Segregation in USForeignRelations. http://www.africaaction.org/featdocs/afr2003.htm
Hope For Africa. *Newsweek*. July 14, 2003.
Sources for International Fan Club:

Nelson Mandela quoted from CBS News. January 30, 2003.
Makiko Tanaka quoted in "Japanese Foreign Minister Tanaka Makes Inappropriate Private Remark About Bush", *The Weekly Post*. June 25, 2001- July 1, 2001.
Francie Ducros quoted from *The Daily Telegraph*. March 6, 2003.
Herta Daeubler-Gmelin quoted from *The Exile*. October 16, 2002.
Carolyn Parrish quoted from CBS News. February 27, 2003.

Source for Mini-Nukes "Yes":
John Holum. Don't Make Mini-Nukes. *International Herald Tribune*. June 9, 2003
Sources for Mini-Nukes "No":
William Laurence quoted in Marilyn French, *The War Against Women*.
See also Lawrence Wittner. *Cold War America: From Hiroshima to Watergate*.
Helen Caldicott. *Missile Envy - The Arms Race and Nuclear War*.
Alexander Cockburn. *Al Gore - A User's Manual*, and: http://www.washingtonpost.com/ac2/wp-dyn?pagename=article&node=&contentId=A32530-2003Feb19&notFound=true

Sources for "We Shall Meet Them in the Malls....":
Shopping is Patriotic, Leaders Say. *National Post Online*, September 28, 2001.

Chapter 7
Sources for More Collected Wisdom:

[A] "society that has romanticized violence."
J. H. Hatfield.. *Fortunate Son*.p. 89.
"Some people think it's inappropriate . . . "
Source: J. H. Hatfield, *Fortunate Son*, p. 285
"I gave them [the Taliban] a fair chance."
Milan Rai, "War Plan - *Ten Reasons Against War on Iraq*, p. 38.
"Whether we bring our enemies to justice or bring justice to our enemies, justice will be done."
Speech. Joint Session of Congress, September 20, 2001.
"Kim Jong Il is a pygmy."

Newsweek www.msnbc.com/news/754330.asp.

"I loathe Kim Jong Il."

Bob Woodward. *Bush At War*, p. 340.

"I hope this [Iraq situation] will not require military action."

Bob Woodward. *Bush At War*, p. 350.

"I'm the Commander see…"

Bob Woodward. *Bush at War*.

"We must apply our conservative and free-market ideas . . ."

J. H. Hatfield.. *Fortunate Son*, p. 236.

"Thousands of dangerous killers . . ."

Source: 2003 State of the Union Address.

"These [terrorist] enemies view the entire world as a battlefield." 2003 State of the Union Address.

"America has no empire to extend . . ."

Speech at West Point, June 1, 2002.

"I admire the strong leadership of President Musharraf."

2003 State of the Union Address.

"Dead or Alive"

Bob Woodward. *Bush At War*, p. 100.

"I looked the man in the eye . . . "

Carolyn B. Thompson and James W. Ware. *The Genius of George W. Bush*, p. 255.

"This CRUSADE, this war on terrorism is going to take a while."

Bob Woodward. *Bush At War*, p. 94.

[A] pretty good political handbook."

J. H. Hatfield. *Fortunate Son*, p. 235.

Sources for "Seizing the Moral Highground":

William Blum. *Rogue State*: *A Guide To The World's Only Superpower*.

Noam Chomsky. *Rogue States*.

Michael Klare. *Rogue States and Nuclear Outlaws*.

Howard Zinn. *A People's History of the United States*.

Chapter 8

Source for "Help George Stop Evil Before It Starts":
Gore Vidal paraphrased from his May 4, 2003. talk to New York Society For Ethical Culture in New York City.

Sources for Total Safety Through Total Police

Power :

Jesse Berney. The beginning of the end for the Constitution? November 24, 2001. www.wageslave.org

Barbara Olshansky and the Center For Constitutional Rights, *Secret Trials and Executions - Military Tribunals and the Threat To Democracy* p. 7, 15, 16, 17, 18, 21, 22, 23, 24, 25, 26, 27, 29, 30, 31, 33.

For the Rumsfeld quote, see Norman Solomon and Reese Erlich, *Target Iraq*: *What The News Media Didn't Tell You*, p. 97.

Source for "Tax Cuts Breed More Patriotic Americans" These parents give from heart to help fund Eugene school. *The Oregonian*. April 22, 2003.

Chapter 9

Sources for 7 Habits:

V. G. Kiernan. *The Lords Of Human Kind - European Attitudes to the Outside World in the Imperial Age*.

Edward Said. *Culture And Imperialism*.

Noam Chomsky. *Year 501 - The Conquest Continues*.

Noam Chomsky. *Deterring Democracy*.

Richard Drinnon. *Facing West: The Metaphysics of Indian Hating and Empire Building*.

David F. Schmitz. *Thank God They're On Our Side - The United States & Right-Wing Dictatorships*.

Eduardo Galeano. *Memory of Fire, Vol. 2*.

Daniel Schirmer. *Republic or Empire - American Resistance to the Philippine War*.

"Living conditions still dire: UN" May 5, 2003. www.new.com.au

Paranjo Guha Thakurta. Reconstructing Iraq: Crony capitalism at its worst. April 29, 2003. www.rediff.com

Index

ABOUT THE AUTHORS ────────────────────────────────▶

The author of *Portraits of Empire: Unmasking Imperial Illusions from the "American Century" to the "War on Terror,"* Michael K. Smith is a dissident historian from the San Francisco Bay Area. He has spent a number of years studying and working abroad, including stays in Mexico, revolutionary Nicaragua, and corporate Japan.

─────────────────────

Matt Wuerker is a freelance cartoonist whose work is published widely in publications that range from *Funny Times* and Jim Hightower's *The Lowdown* to *The Nation* , *The Washington Post*, and *The Christian Science Monitor*.

The last collection of his cartoons, *Meanwhile in Other News.... A Graphic Look at Politics in the Empire of Money, Sex and Scandal*, was published by Common Courage Press in 1998. His work is also included in the anthology: "Attitude— the New Subversive Cartoonists" (Edited by Ted Rall, NRB Publishers, 2002).

◀────────────────────────────────▶